READER'S DIGEST

A Passion for Pasta

Eat Well

READER'S DIGEST

A Passion
for Pasta

Published by The Reader's Digest Association Limited
London • New York • Sydney • Montreal

A PASSION FOR PASTA is part of a series of cookery books called
EAT WELL LIVE WELL and was created by Amazon Publishing Limited.

Series Editor *Norma MacMillan*
Volume Editor *Bridget Jones*
Art Director *Bobbie Colgate Stone*
Photographic Direction *Bobbie Colgate Stone*
Designer *Giles Powell-Smith*
Editorial Assistants *Zoe Lehmann, Anna Ward*
Proofreader *Alison Leach*
Nutritionists *Fiona Hunter BSc Hons (Nutri.), Dip. Dietetics,
Jane Thomas BSc, M Med Sci, SRD*

CONTRIBUTORS
Writers *Sara Buenfeld, Anne Gains, Carole Handslip,
Beverly LeBlanc, Janette Marshall, Jenni Muir, Marlena Spieler*
Recipe Testers *Bridget Colvin, Anne Gains, Clare Lewis,
Heather Owen, Maggie Pannell, Susanna Tee*
Recipe Testing Co-ordinator *Anne Gains*
Photographer *Martin Brigdale*
Stylist *Helen Trent*
Home Economists *Maxine Clark, Bridget Sargeson*

FOR READER'S DIGEST
Series Editor *Christine Noble*
Editorial Assistant *Caroline Boucher*
Production Controllers *Kathy Brown, Jane Holyer*

READER'S DIGEST GENERAL BOOKS
Editorial Director *Cortina Butler*
Art Director *Nick Clark*

ISBN 0 276 42422 0

First Edition Copyright © 1999
The Reader's Digest Association Limited
11 Westferry Circus, Canary Wharf, London E14 4HE

Copyright © 1999 Reader's Digest Association Far East Limited
Philippines copyright © 1999 Reader's Digest Association Far East Limited

Reprinted with amendments 2000

Notes for the reader
• Use all metric or all imperial measures when preparing a recipe,
as the two sets of measurements are not exact equivalents.
• Recipes were tested using metric measures and conventional
(not fan-assisted) ovens. Medium eggs were used, unless
otherwise specified.
• Can sizes are approximate, as weights can vary slightly
according to the manufacturer.
• Preparation and cooking times are only intended as a guide.

The nutritional information in this book is for reference only.
The editors urge anyone with continuing medical problems or
symptoms to consult a doctor.

Contents

6 Introduction

Eating well to live well

8 Perfect Pasta

26 Pasta First

Eating well to live well

Eating a healthy diet can help you look good, feel great and have lots of energy. Nutrition fads come and go, but the simple keys to eating well remain the same: enjoy a variety of food – no single food contains all the vitamins, minerals, fibre and other essential components you need for health and vitality – and get the balance right by looking at the proportions of the different foods you eat. Add some regular exercise too – at least 30 minutes a day, 3 times a week – and you'll be helping yourself to live well and make the most of your true potential.

Getting it into proportion

Current guidelines are that most people in the UK should eat more starchy foods, more fruit and vegetables, and less fat, meat products and sugary foods. It is almost impossible to give exact amounts that you should eat, as every single person's requirements vary, depending on size, age and the amount of energy expended during the day. However, the Health Education Authority has suggested an ideal balance of the different foods that provide us with energy (calories) and the nutrients needed for health. The number of daily portions of each of the food groups will vary from person to person – for example, an active teenager might need to eat up to 14 portions of starchy carbohydrates every day, whereas a sedentary adult would only require 6 or 7 portions – but the proportions of the food groups in relation to each other should ideally stay the same.

More detailed explanations of food groups and nutritional terms can be found on pages 156–158, together with brief guidelines on amounts which can be used in conjunction with the nutritional analyses of the recipes. A simple way to get the balance right, however, is to imagine a daily 'plate' divided into the different food groups. On the imaginary 'plate', starchy carbohydrates fill at least one-third of the space, thus constituting the main part of your meals. Fruit and vegetables fill the same amount of space. The remaining third of the 'plate' is divided mainly between protein foods and dairy foods, with just a little space allowed for foods containing fat and sugar. These are the proportions to aim for.

It isn't essential to eat the ideal proportions on the 'plate' at every meal, or even every day – balancing them over a week or two is just as good. The healthiest diet for you and your family is one that is generally balanced and sustainable in the long term.

Our daily plate
Starchy carbohydrate foods: eat 6–14 portions a day

At least 50% of the calories in a healthy diet should come from carbohydrates, and most of that from starchy foods – bread, potatoes and other starchy vegetables, pasta, rice and cereals. For most people in the UK this means doubling current intake. Starchy carbohydrates are the best foods for energy. They also provide protein and essential vitamins and minerals, particularly those from the B group. Eat a variety of starchy foods, choosing wholemeal or wholegrain types whenever possible, because the fibre they contain helps to prevent constipation, bowel disease, heart disease and other health problems.

What is a portion of starchy foods?
Some examples are: 3 tbsp breakfast cereal • 2 tbsp muesli • 1 slice of bread or toast • 1 bread roll, bap or bun • 1 small pitta bread, naan bread or chapatti • 3 crackers or crispbreads • 1 medium-sized potato • 1 medium-sized plantain or small sweet potato • 2 heaped tbsp boiled rice • 2 heaped tbsp boiled pasta.

Fruit and vegetables: eat at least 5 portions a day

Nutrition experts are unanimous that we would all benefit from eating more fruit and vegetables each day – a total of at least 400 g (14 oz) of fruit and vegetables (edible part) is the target. Fruit and vegetables provide vitamin C for immunity and healing, and other 'antioxidant' vitamins and minerals for protection against cardiovascular disease and cancer. They also offer several 'phytochemicals' that help protect against cancer, and B vitamins, especially folate, which is important for women planning a pregnancy, to prevent birth defects. All of these, plus other nutrients, work together to boost well-being.

Antioxidant nutrients (e.g. vitamins C and beta-carotene, which are mainly derived from fruit and vegetables) and vitamin E help to prevent harmful free radicals in the body initiating or accelerating cancer, heart disease, cataracts, arthritis, general ageing, sun damage to skin, and damage to sperm. Free radicals occur naturally as a by-product of normal cell function, but are also caused by pollutants such as tobacco smoke and over-exposure to sunlight.

What is a portion of fruit or vegetables?
Some examples are: 1 medium-sized portion of vegetables or salad • 1 medium-sized piece of fresh fruit • 6 tbsp (about 140 g/5 oz) stewed or canned fruit • 1 small glass (100 ml/3½ fl oz) fruit juice.

Dairy foods: eat 2–3 portions a day

Dairy foods, such as milk, cheese, yogurt and fromage frais, are the best source of calcium for strong bones and teeth, and important for the nervous system. They also provide some protein for growth and repair, vitamin B_{12}, and vitamin A for healthy eyes. They are particularly valuable foods for young children, who need full-fat versions at least up to age 2. Dairy foods are also especially important for adolescent girls to prevent the development of osteoporosis later in life, and for women throughout life generally.

To limit fat intake, wherever possible adults should choose lower-fat dairy foods, such as semi-skimmed milk and low-fat yogurt.

What is a portion of dairy foods?
Some examples are: 1 medium-sized glass (200 ml/7 fl oz) milk • 1 matchbox-sized piece (40 g/1½ oz) Cheddar cheese • 1 small pot of yogurt • 125 g (4½ oz) cottage cheese or fromage frais.

Protein foods: eat 2–4 portions a day

Lean meat, fish, eggs and vegetarian alternatives provide protein for growth and cell repair, as well as iron to prevent anaemia. Meat also provides B vitamins for healthy nerves and digestion, especially vitamin B_{12}, and zinc for growth and healthy bones and skin. Only moderate amounts of these protein-rich foods are required. An adult woman needs about 45 g of protein a day and an adult man 55 g, which constitutes about 11% of a day's calories. This is less than the current average intake. For optimum health, we need to eat some protein every day.

What is a portion of protein-rich food?

Some examples are: 3 medium-sized slices (50–70 g/scant 2–3 oz) beef, pork, ham, lamb, liver, kidney, chicken or oily fish • 115–140 g (4–5 oz) white fish (not fried in batter) • 3 fish fingers • 2 eggs (up to 4 a week) • 5 tbsp (200 g/7 oz) baked beans or other pulses or lentils • 2 tbsp (60 g/2¼ oz) nuts, peanut butter or other nut products.

Foods containing fat: 1–5 portions per day

Unlike fruit, vegetables and starchy carbohydrates, which can be eaten in abundance, fatty foods should not exceed 33% of the day's calories in a balanced diet, and only 10% of this should be from saturated fat. This quantity of fat may seem a lot, but it isn't – fat contains more than twice as many calories per gram as either carbohydrate or protein.

Overconsumption of fat is a major cause of weight and health problems. A healthy diet must contain a certain amount of fat to provide fat-soluble vitamins and essential fatty acids, needed for the development and function of the brain, eyes and nervous system, but we only need a small amount each day – just 25 g is required, which is much less than we consume in our Western diet. The current recommendations from the Department of Health are a maximum of 75 g fat (of this, 21.5 g saturated) for women each day and 99 g fat (28.5 g saturated) for men. The best sources of the essential fatty acids are natural fish oils and pure vegetable oils.

What is a portion of fatty foods?

Some examples are: 1 tsp butter or margarine • 2 tsp low-fat spread • 1 tsp cooking oil • 1 tbsp mayonnaise or vinaigrette (salad dressing) • 1 tbsp cream • 1 individual packet of crisps.

Foods containing sugar: 0–2 portions per day

Although many foods naturally contain sugars (e.g. fruit contains fructose, milk lactose), health experts recommend that we limit 'added' sugars. Added sugars, such as table sugar, provide only calories – they contain no vitamins, minerals or fibre to contribute to health, and it is not necessary to eat them at all. But, as the old adage goes, 'a little of what you fancy does you good' and sugar is no exception. Denial of foods, or using them as rewards or punishment, is not a healthy attitude to eating, and can lead to cravings, binges and yo-yo dieting. Sweet foods are a pleasurable part of a well-balanced diet, but added sugars should account for no more than 11% of the total daily carbohydrate intake.

In assessing how much sugar you consume, don't forget that it is a major ingredient of many processed and ready-prepared foods.

What is a portion of sugary foods?

Some examples are: 3 tsp sugar • 1 heaped tsp jam or honey • 2 biscuits • half a slice of cake • 1 doughnut • 1 Danish pastry • 1 small bar of chocolate • 1 small tube or bag of sweets.

Too salty

Salt (sodium chloride) is essential for a variety of body functions, but we tend to eat too much through consumption of salty processed foods, 'fast' foods and ready-prepared foods, and by adding salt in cooking and at the table. The end result can be rising blood pressure as we get older, which puts us at higher risk of heart disease and stroke. Eating more vegetables and fruit increases potassium intake, which can help to counteract the damaging effects of salt.

Alcohol in a healthy diet

In recent research, moderate drinking of alcohol has been linked with a reduced risk of heart disease and stroke among men and women over 45. However, because of other risks associated with alcohol, particularly in excess quantities, no doctor would recommend taking up drinking if you are teetotal. The healthiest pattern of drinking is to enjoy small amounts of alcohol with food, to have alcohol-free days and always to avoid getting drunk. A well-balanced diet is vital because nutrients from food (vitamins and minerals) are needed to detoxify the alcohol.

Water – the best choice

Drinking plenty of non-alcoholic liquid each day is an often overlooked part of a well-balanced diet. A minimum of 8 glasses (which is about 2 litres/3½ pints) is the ideal. If possible, these should not all be tea or coffee, as these are stimulants and diuretics, which cause the body to lose liquids, taking with them water-soluble vitamins. Water is the best choice. Other good choices are fruit or herb teas or tisanes, fruit juices – diluted with water, if preferred – or semi-skimmed milk (full-fat milk for very young children). Fizzy sugary or acidic drinks such as cola are more likely to damage tooth enamel than other drinks.

As a guide to the vitamin and mineral content of foods and recipes in the book, we have used the following terms and symbols, based on the percentage of the daily RNI provided by one serving for the average adult man or woman aged 19–49 years (see also pages 156–158):

✓✓✓ *or* excellent   at least 50% (half)

✓✓ *or* good   25–50% (one-quarter to one-half)

✓ *or* useful   10–25% (one-tenth to one-quarter)

Note that recipes contribute other nutrients, but the analyses only include those that provide at least 10% RNI per portion. Vitamins and minerals where deficiencies are rare are not included.

Ⓥ denotes that a recipe is suitable for vegetarians.

Perfect Pasta

Every bit as nutritious as it is delicious

PASTA IS THE PERFECT FOOD for a modern healthy diet, being low in fat and calories and high in starchy carbohydrates and vitamins. And it is so versatile – ideal for everyday eating as well as easily transformed into dishes to suit any occasion. No wonder pasta is loved all over the world. You can buy it dried or fresh, in hundreds of different shapes, sizes and even flavours. Even better, make and shape pasta dough yourself, colouring it to surprise and delight family and friends. Cooking pasta is as simple as boiling water, and there is a vast choice of delicious sauces to dress it, from the simplest tomato or pesto to wild mushrooms, seafood and truffles.

Pasta in a healthy diet

One of the world's most popular foods, enjoyed equally by families who want healthy meals in a hurry and by gourmets who toss it with truffles, pasta is a perfect staple for high-vitality, healthy eating. There is an enormous variety of pasta shapes and myriad delicious sauces for everyday eating and special occasions.

Why eat pasta?

Pasta has an ideal 'healthy eating' profile in that it is a low-fat, starchy (complex carbohydrate) food. Starchy carbohydrates should make up at least half of the daily calories in a well-balanced diet. Adding more pasta to meals is one of the easiest, most varied and nutritious ways to increase your starchy food intake.

There is a popular myth that pasta is fattening, but with the right sauces and accompaniments, the opposite is true – pasta is relatively low in calories and it helps to control hunger by making us feel full, leaving less room for fatty foods which are more likely to cause weight problems. Regular physical exercise in combination with a diet based around starchy carbohydrates is the best way to maintain a healthy waistline.

Does it all add up?

While the human body is less likely to turn starchy carbohydrates into body fat than it is fatty foods, eating too much carbohydrate can cause a weight gain. Each gram of carbohydrate – starch or sugar – provides 4 kcal. So if you want to increase the starchy food in your diet, be sure that the quantity of calories eaten still matches the calories used up.

Great shape from simple grain

Pasta is traditionally made from durum wheat semolina. Durum wheat, grown in Italy, the Middle East and North America, is a 'hard' wheat with a high gluten content. Gluten is a protein that gives flour its strength and elasticity, which is what enables pasta dough to be rolled and shaped.

Pasta dough may be made from just flour, water and salt, or eggs or oil may be added to enrich the dough. Vegetable purées are used to colour pasta, but they are not present in sufficient quantity to make a major nutritional contribution.

Pasta can be made from a mixture of flour and durum semolina or standard wheat flour. Flours from other grains, such as buckwheat, rice or beans, are also used to make pasta – useful for people who cannot eat wheat or gluten.

Semolina is used to make gnocchi (small dumplings) and rolled into couscous. Couscous is a traditional North African staple, served in much the same way as pasta, to partner poultry, meat or vegetable stews and sauces.

Essential fibre

In addition to helping to control hunger pangs and reducing the likelihood of weight problems, diets rich in starchy foods have other plus points. Undigested fibre in starchy food passes to the colon, where it ferments and stimulates the production of healthy gut bacteria. These 'friendly bacteria' aid digestion and outnumber potentially harmful bacteria. This 'biomass' of good gut bacteria also helps to bulk faeces, preventing constipation and associated problems, such as piles.

The fermentation of the fibre produces fatty acids, which offer health benefits such as helping to regulate cell growth in the intestine, giving protection against colon cancer.

Brilliant for B vitamins

Pasta contains valuable vitamins, most notably B vitamins. B vitamins are water-soluble, and not stored for long in the body, so we need to eat them regularly. They are essential for healthy digestion and for the steady

wholemeal flour and farfalle

buckwheat flour and fusilli

pasta *all'uova* is enriched with eggs

wheat flour, eggs, oil and salt

semolina gnocchi

couscous

and continuous release of energy from starchy foods. They are also important for healthy nerves, mental activity and memory. In particular, B_1 (thiamin) is needed to help to convert protein into muscle; B_2 (riboflavin), niacin and B_6 to convert food into energy; and B_6 for the creation of red blood cells and to prevent anaemia. All pasta provides B vitamins, although wholemeal varieties have more than white pasta, and in addition contain vitamin E from the germ of the wheat grain.

A source of minerals
Wholemeal pasta offers zinc and iron, essential to prevent anaemia. Selenium (mainly found in wholemeal pasta) is, like zinc, an antioxidant needed to make enzymes that destroy harmful free radicals, a by-product of normal cell function. Antioxidant nutrients prevent free radicals initiating cancer, heart disease and other health problems.

Pasta power
Athletes appreciate the value of pasta: most elite athletes eat a high-carbohydrate diet for a few days before an event, plus a starchy pre-event meal to boost energy and endurance. This is called carbohydrate loading. The body turns starch into glucose and glycogen, which is stored in muscles and liver, producing a better source of energy than sugar.

For most of us carbohydrate loading is unnecessary, but we can eat starchy food after exercise (as opposed to sugary or fatty food) to replenish depleted energy effectively.

Pasta and energy – the GI factor
GI stands for Glycaemic Index, which is a ranking of foods based on their effect on blood sugar levels. Low-GI foods break down slowly, releasing energy gradually into the bloodstream, which results in a smaller rise of blood sugar. High-GI foods cause a larger rise of blood sugar. Low-GI foods are more desirable because they can help to control hunger, appetite and weight, and lower raised blood fats. Pasta is a low-GI food, and the less processing during manufacture the lower the score: wholemeal pasta has a lower GI than white pasta, and thicker shapes score lower than thin varieties.

perfect pasta

Know your pasta – Italian style

With literally hundreds of varieties of pasta, healthy meals need never become boring. When planning a menu, instead of emphasising the protein element, try choosing the pasta first and make it the largest portion of food on the plate. Then add lots of vegetables and a smaller quantity of fish, poultry or meat in the sauce.

A pasta primer

Buying pasta can be quite an adventure – plain or filled, white, wholemeal or multi-coloured, big or small? Pasta comes in an almost bewildering variety of shapes and sizes, and many have several names that may be simply regional or peculiar to a particular manufacturer. Here are some helpful Italian terms.

• *Pasta di semola grano duro* indicates that it is made from durum wheat flour, and *all'uova* that it is enriched with eggs.

• The word endings to pasta names can indicate the size of the shape: *oni* is large, for example conchiglioni (large shells); *ette* or *etti* are small, as in spaghetti, cappelletti (small hats) or orecchiette (small ears); and *ini* are smaller still.

• Spinach makes pasta *verde* (green); beetroot makes pasta *alla bietola* or *rossi* (red); and squid ink is added to make pasta *seppia* or *neroli* (black).

Although the description 'fresh' implies greater nutritional status, both fresh and dried pasta offer the same benefits.

Shaping up

Campanelle are bells with frilly edges, as are ballerine.

Capelli d'angelo, which literally means 'angel hair', are long and extremely thin strands.

Cannelloni are large tubes that are filled and baked.

Casarecce are rolled lengths forming an s-shape at each end.

Conchiglie are shells; conchigliette are a smaller version, while conchiglie grande are jumbo ones for stuffing.

Ditali are thimbles or tubes; ditalini are very small ones.

Farfalle are in the shape of bows, also described as bow ties or butterflies. Small bows are farfallette or farfallini.

Fettuccine are long, flat ribbons, about 5 mm (¼ in) wide.

Fusilli are spirals or corkscrews, also called coils or springs. They may be long or short. Another name for these is rotini.

Gemelli are narrow spirals or twists with hollow ends.

Gnocchi are fluted shells. Another name for these is cavatelli.

Lasagne are flat rectangular or square sheets. Lasagnette are wide, flat noodles with ruffled edges; reginette are similar.

Linguine are long, flat ribbon noodles, thinner than fettuccine.

Lumache are described as snail-shaped.

Macaroni are smooth, thick tubes. They may be as long as spaghetti, or 'short-cut' and straight or curved (elbow macaroni). Cavatappi are ridged spiral macaroni.

Orecchiette are small ear shapes.

Pappardelle are flat noodles about 2 cm (¾ in) wide.

Penne are short, straight tubes, cut diagonally to give them quill-like ends. They may be ridged (penne rigati) or smooth.

Radiatori look like little grills.

Rigatoni are short, ridged tubes, fatter than penne.

Spaghetti, the most familiar form of pasta outside Italy, are long, string-like strands. Spaghettini are thinner.

Tagliatelle are long, flat ribbon noodles, like fettuccine.

Vermicelli are a finer version of spaghetti.

Well filled

Filled pasta can be bought dried, but fresh is superior – the flavour and quality of dried stuffed pasta, particularly the filling, can be disappointing. These are the classic shapes.

Agnolotti are rectangular or crescent-shaped envelopes, traditionally filled with meat.

Capelletti are small stuffed hat-shaped pasta.

Ravioli are small or large square, round or oval parcels.

Tortelloni are large stuffed squares.

Tortellini are little stuffed rings, made by folding circles or squares in half, then pinching the corners together.

capelli d'angelo

conchiglie

cannelloni

fresh linguine

vermicelli

farfalle

dried linguine

pappardelle

penne

capelletti

fettuccine

fusilli

ravioli

tortellini

agnolotti

tagliatelle

rigatoni

tortelloni

Oriental and non-wheat pasta

Chinese cooks may not have invented noodles – Marco Polo knew about pasta before he went to the Orient – but they certainly spread the healthy habit of eating noodles throughout the Far East. Filled pasta also features, with spring rolls and the little dumplings called wontons concealing portions of succulent fillings.

Noodles for breakfast

Noodle is the name given to flat ribbons of pasta (Italian and other types) and it is also applied to some round varieties. In the Orient, noodles are made from the staple grain of the region; for example, there are rice or buckwheat noodles, and even noodles made from mung or soya beans and vegetables. Dumpling wrappers are also a type of pasta dough.

Noodles are not confined to main meals. In Japan, for example, small local noodle restaurants, bars and stalls in towns and villages serve a wide variety of nutritious hot and cold vegetarian and non-vegetarian noodle dishes from breakfast through lunch and well into the evening. Similar enthusiasm for noodles exists in Malaysia, Thailand, Indonesia, Vietnam, Korea and the Philippines, where traditional meals incorporate noodles as a basic starchy food in a diet rich in vegetables and fruit.

Health bites

Oriental noodles are every bit as nutritious as other types of pasta, with specific benefits depending on the grain from which they are made. Many non-wheat noodles are gluten-free, which makes them a suitable starchy food for people intolerant of wheat or gluten, also found in barley and rye.

Remember that crispy noodles, popular in fast-food and take-away restaurants, absorb a lot of oil or animal fat during deep-frying, so enjoy them now and again rather than every day.

Oriental noodle know-how

Cellophane noodles, also called transparent or bean thread noodles, are made from ground mung beans. These fine, white noodles are sold dried, in bundles. Before being added to soups or other dishes, they are soaked in water or stock, which makes them slippery and translucent.

Rice noodles, in China, are made from a mixture of rice flour, wheat starch and water. There are very fine, string-like noodles, sometimes called rice vermicelli, which are often broken up for use in soups, or deep-fried which causes them to puff up dramatically. Rice sticks are flat noodles, sometimes only about the length of a chopstick. They are most often served in a broth or sauce. Somen are fine rice noodles from Japan, used mainly in soup.

Soba, brown in colour, are the best-known Japanese noodles. Made from buckwheat flour, they are quite substantial – like wholemeal pasta – and are often served with a dipping sauce.

Spring rolls and egg rolls are made using slightly opaque, paper-thin wrappers. Chinese spring roll wrappers are made from wheat flour; the Vietnamese version is based on rice flour. Spring roll and rice paper wrappers may be bought frozen (thaw before use) or you can buy the prepared spring rolls. Try baking them on non-stick baking trays instead of deep-frying, for a low-fat result.

Wheat noodles, made from wheat flour and often enriched with egg, can be bought fresh or dried, in a wide variety of widths, flat or round. They need very little cooking – often just soaking. The Japanese have their own version of Chinese-style wheat noodles, called ramen.

Wonton wrappers, pale yellow in colour, are made from a wheat flour and egg dough. The small square or round wrappers are available fresh or frozen, and can be used to make wontons as well as other dumplings such as dim sum or

Japanese noodles

Preparing and cooking

Most Oriental noodles are either soaked or cooked in boiling water before being added to soups, vegetable dishes or stir-fries. They can also be served with a sauce, as for Italian-style pasta, or as a side dish. Noodle stir-fries, with lots of fresh vegetables and a moderate amount of lean meat, fish, shellfish, tofu or beans, make extremely well-balanced meals.

Alternative grains for making pasta

There is a wide range of Italian-style pasta made from grains other than wheat, including corn, barley, rice, soya-bean flour and vegetables. Combinations such as rice and soya-bean flours provide a good source of vegetarian protein and fibre. Many of these products are found in large supermarkets and healthfood shops as well as from mail-order suppliers.

cellophane noodles   Chinese wheat noodles

spring rolls

rice noodles

wonton wrappers

pot-stickers. Once filled, the dumplings can be fried, boiled or steamed (a good low-fat choice), or used in soup. Traditional wonton stuffings include pork, prawns and mushrooms.

Buying and storing Oriental noodles

Fresh noodles can be stored in their unopened packet in the fridge for up to 3 days. They can also be frozen: open freeze them on a tray and pack in freezer boxes or bags when hard, so that small quantities can be cooked from frozen as required. Check 'use by' dates on the packets before buying.

Dried noodles should be stored as for other types of dried pasta. Once opened, store in an airtight container. Check 'best before' dates before buying.

Buying and cooking pasta

Pasta is an excellent food for busy people, not only for speedy cooking, but also because it can always be to hand – dried types have a long shelf life and fresh pasta is the perfect freezer-standby food. For hassle-free healthy eating, think 'pasta' when planning your shopping.

Buying tips

- Often the tastiest fresh pasta and the largest range of unusual dried shapes are available from Italian food shops, so if you have one near you, check it out.
- Check the 'best before' dates on packs of dried pasta. Unlike 'use by' dates on highly perishable food, it is not illegal to sell goods that are older than the 'best before' dates. However, the quality will probably have deteriorated. Try to buy from a store with a good turnover of stock.
- For everyday or frequent eating, look for stuffed pasta shapes that are lowest in fat. The best-quality fillings are those containing mainly the key ingredient; for example, on a packet of ricotta and spinach ravioli, the ricotta and spinach should be the first two ingredients listed. A long list of other ingredients, such as modified starches, water or other 'fillers' and additives, tends to indicate that the filling contains less of the main ingredient(s).

- Examine the pasta in the pack closely and choose shapes that look as though they have a generous amount of filling.
- As a general guide, bought fresh pasta with a low-fat filling, such as mushroom and garlic, will contain not more than 5 g fat per 100 g (3½ oz). This information is given on the nutritional labelling panel on the packet.
- Long-life products, such as vacuum-packed stuffed pasta shapes, tend to have a less pleasing flavour than fresh pasta.

Storing pasta

After opening, store any unused dried pasta in an airtight container. Cut the 'best before' date off the packet and put it in the container for future reference. Keep in a cool, dry place.

Store fresh pasta in the fridge. Once a packet is opened, use it within 2 days, or freeze any unused pasta in freezer bags or an airtight container; it will keep for up to 8 months. If the pasta pieces are large, open freeze them on a tray covered with

leftover dried pasta keeps well
in airtight jars

fresh pasta is a useful freezer standby

cling film, then transfer them to a freezer bag or container once they are hard. This keeps pieces separate, so that the required number can be removed very easily. Cook pasta from frozen for about 3 minutes.

Cooking pasta

- Use a large pan so that the pasta can move freely in the boiling water.
- Bring the pan of water to the boil, allowing 1 litre (1¾ pints) water to every 100 g (3½ oz) pasta.
- If using salt, add it to the water before adding the pasta. It is not necessary to add oil to the water, except for lasagne sheets which are more likely to stick together.
- Add the pasta to the boiling water. Cover the pan until the water comes back to the boil, then remove the lid. Stir once to prevent the pasta from sticking together.
- Once the pasta is cooked, drain in a large colander. If serving the pasta hot, do not rinse as this washes off the starch that gives taste and texture. Occasionally, pasta is rinsed before use in salads or baked dishes, such as lasagne.
- Save some cooking water to dress pasta or to thin sauces.

The question of salt

Many cooks recommend adding 1 tsp coarse sea salt to every 1 litre (1¾ pints) water when cooking pasta. However, as pasta already contains salt, and reducing salt intake is often a step towards improving the diet, you may wish to use less. If you gradually reduce the amount of salt used in your cooking and eating, you will give your palate time to adjust to less salty food.

Cooking times

Check and follow packet instructions as cooking times vary, particularly for Oriental noodles and specialist non-wheat pasta. Typically, Italian-style dried white and coloured pasta takes 8–12 minutes to cook and wholemeal pasta 12–15 minutes, depending on size and thickness. The pasta is ready when it is al dente – tender but still firm, offering some resistance when bitten. At this stage, some cooks add a cup of cold water before draining to halt the cooking.

Fresh pasta, bought or home-made, cooks very quickly – usually in 3–5 minutes, although some types are cooked in just 1 minute.

Pasta portions

As a general guide, for a pasta dish with a light dressing or sauce, allow 50 g (1¾ oz) dried pasta and 100 g (3½ oz) fresh pasta per person for a light meal or starter, and 85 g (3 oz) dried or 115–150 g (4–5 oz) fresh pasta for a main course. Portions can vary considerably according to the quantities of other ingredients used, especially when lots of satisfying vegetables are served, and according to appetite.

drain pasta well so that sauces won't be watery

simply dressed pasta makes a filling light meal

Making pasta and its sauces

You are sure to be impressed by the superior flavour and texture of home-made pasta. Making the dough allows you to vary the ingredients and flavourings used to produce a pasta that suits your specific requirements. And with a freshly made sauce, you can turn your pasta into a delicious meal to suit any occasion.

Home-made pasta

Pasta is surprisingly simple to make, and once you get the hang of handling the dough, you will be able to experiment with an enormous number of fillings and accompaniments. Making filled pasta also means that you can benefit from the freshest ingredients to boost nutrients and enjoyment.

All you need are a few standard kitchen items – rolling pin, sharp knife and metal pastry cutters. A pastry wheel is useful. If you decide to make pasta regularly, and in quantity, it is worth investing in a pasta machine. Hand-operated machines are very successful, but there are also electric pasta makers and attachments for food processors. Follow the manufacturer's instructions for using a machine.

Ingredients

Flour Some supermarkets and many Italian specialist shops sell special flour for making pasta. The flour may be 100% durum wheat semolina, such as an authentic Italian flour called *doppio zero* (double zero), which appears on the bag as 00 grade. Other flour sold for making pasta may be a combination of durum wheat semolina and ordinary flour.

Alternatively, use unbleached strong plain flour or plain wholemeal flour. A mixture of unbleached strong plain flour and buckwheat or rice flour can also be used. A small portion of soya flour will boost the protein content of the pasta.

Eggs Although much commercial pasta is made with just flour and water, most home-made pasta includes eggs. Standard medium eggs are ideal.

Oil Olive oil is authentic. Since the amount used is small, it will not have a great impact on the fat content of a dish.

Salt Fine sea salt offers the best flavour.

Tips for success

• Flour can vary in absorbency and egg sizes may differ, so results may vary on different occasions even with the same recipe. Weather and humidity also affect the dough.
• Sprinkle strands of freshly cut pasta liberally with semolina or flour to prevent them from sticking together.
• If you do not want to cook the dough immediately, you can freeze it, then cook it from frozen.

Fresh pasta

Makes about 675 g (1¹/₂ lb)
450 g (1 lb) strong plain flour
pinch of salt
4 eggs, beaten
1 tbsp extra virgin olive oil

Preparation time: 45 minutes, plus 30 minutes resting

1 Sift the flour onto a clean work surface or into a large mixing bowl. Make a well in the centre and add the salt, eggs and oil.

2 Using your hands, gradually mix the flour into the eggs and oil, until the mixture begins to form a firm dough. If necessary, add a few drops of water.

3 Knead the dough for about 10 minutes or until it is smooth and elastic. The dough should still be firm. Add a little extra flour if the dough becomes sticky.

4 Wrap the dough tightly in a polythene bag or with cling film and set it aside to rest for 30 minutes before rolling and cutting. Do not place in the fridge.

5 Cut the dough into quarters, as smaller portions are easier to manage. Roll out the dough very thinly on an unfloured surface, turning it over and around occasionally to prevent it from sticking, then cut it into the chosen shapes such as lasagne, cannelloni or noodles.

6 Noodles and unfilled pasta may be cooked immediately or allowed to dry for up to 30 minutes before cooking (see page 17). It is a good idea to leave pasta to dry on clean tea-towels if it is slightly sticky. Hang noodles over a pasta drying rack, or lightly flour them and coil into nests.

Using a food processor

Check the manufacturer's instructions for kneading firm doughs. It is best to use the dough blade attachment. Knead it in the machine for 5–10 minutes.

Cutting simple shapes

Lasagne Cut neat rectangles or squares 7.5–10 cm (3–4 in) wide, or to fit the baking dish.

Cannelloni Instead of buying tubes, cut rectangles or squares and roll them around the filling – make your cannelloni small or chunky and long, as you wish.

Noodles Flour the rolled-out dough, fold it over several times or roll it loosely, and then cut it across into slices. Thin slices give fine noodles; thick slices make wide noodles. Experiment with all widths, from skewer-fine to noodles as wide as a ruler. Carefully unravel the noodles with your fingers.

Squares and diamonds Cut strips, then, without moving them, cut across to make squares or diamond shapes (cut at an angle to make the slanting sides).

Storing freshly made pasta

Leave the pasta to dry for 30 minutes to prevent the pieces from sticking together, then put in a polythene bag or covered container in the fridge. Use within 24 hours. To freeze the pasta for longer storage, spread the pasta out on a tray covered with cling film and open freeze until firm, then pack in polythene bags.

squid ink pasta

spinach ravioli

herb tagliatelle

black olive paste, sun-dried tomato and pesto flavoured pasta

beetroot pasta

saffron pasta

Flavouring pasta dough

Pasta can be coloured and flavoured with a wide variety of vegetable purées and pastes, such as tomato (and sun-dried versions), spinach, beetroot and carrot. Squid ink (available in packets from specialist outlets) can turn pasta dramatically black. Fresh and dried herbs, saffron, ground peppercorns, black olive paste, garlic, wholegrain mustard and spices such as cumin and curry powder can also be added to make interesting pasta.

Spinach Wash 225 g (8 oz) fresh spinach and place in a large saucepan. Cover and cook over a high heat, shaking the pan, for about 3 minutes. (The water clinging to the leaves is sufficient moisture in which to cook the spinach.) Drain well in a sieve, then chop finely or purée in a blender or food processor. Press out all excess water in a sieve, to give a thick paste. Use only 2 eggs for the dough. Add the spinach with the eggs and oil, then mix in the flour as in the basic recipe.

Beetroot Purée 1–2 small cooked beetroot. Use only 3 eggs for the pasta dough, and add the beetroot purée with the eggs.

Herbs Add a handful of finely chopped fresh herbs when mixing in the flour. Flat-leaf parsley, coriander, basil, oregano, marjoram and thyme are all delicious.

Saffron Add 1 tsp powdered saffron or a pinch of saffron threads infused in 1 tbsp boiling water.

Pesto sauce, sun-dried tomato paste or black olive paste Omit the oil and add 2 tbsp of the chosen sauce or paste.

Pasta saucery

The secret of pasta versatility is its compatability with almost any other ingredient. From extravagant seafood to humble herbs and vegetables, sauces served with pasta can reflect all cooking styles. With only a few basic ingredients, a dressing can be conjured up to turn pasta into a delicious meal for every occasion.

In Italy, sauces for pasta were traditionally a celebration of regional produce, both the luxurious and common-or-garden. From truffles and fabulous wild fungi in the north, and aromatic pesto in Genoa, to fish and seafood in the south, and glowing tomatoes in Naples, there are plenty of authentic options. Today, pasta sauces are a vibrant reflection of the wide variety of fresh ingredients available from all over the world. With Mediterranean vegetables matched by spices and flavourings from the Orient, modern pasta sauces are a fashionable fusion food.

A little sauce with a positive zing

The pasta should definitely be the main attraction. The ideal amount of sauce (to Italians and healthy eaters) is enough to coat the pasta lightly without leaving a covering or pool on the plate when the pasta has been eaten.

Sauces based mainly on vegetables, with moderate amounts of lean meat, fish or shellfish, and fresh herbs, positively zing with flavour, colour and good nutrition. The vegetables pack a powerful antioxidant punch from their vitamins and minerals to boost and complement the energy-giving pasta.

Which sauce for which pasta?

There are no hard and fast rules – pasta is so good because it is so versatile – but some shapes have an affinity for certain types of sauce.

• Long thin strands of pasta go well with simple sauces, such as pesto, or can be dressed simply with a little butter or oil to keep the strands separate.

• Thicker strands of pasta and ribbon noodles go well with a meat, cheese or creamy sauce or a smooth tomato sauce.

• Tubular pasta, twists, shells and similar shapes go well with chunkier vegetable sauces.

linguine with pesto sauce (see page 23)

pappardelle with a meat sauce (see page 146)

rigatoni with a chunky vegetable sauce (see page 62)

perfect pasta

Fresh tomato sauce

There are many versions of this delicious, indispensable sauce. This one is a basic recipe for fresh tomatoes. Vine-ripened or full-flavoured summer tomatoes are best, but when they are not available, the sauce can be made with canned tomatoes.

Makes about 600 ml (1 pint), to serve 4

2 tbsp extra virgin olive oil

1 large onion, finely chopped

1 garlic clove, chopped

1 kg (2¼ lb) tomatoes, skinned, seeded and chopped

150 ml (5 fl oz) red wine or vegetable stock

2 tbsp chopped fresh basil or 1 tsp dried basil

pinch of sugar

salt and pepper

To serve (optional)

8–10 sprigs of fresh basil, shredded

4 tbsp freshly grated Parmesan cheese or 4 heaped tbsp Parmesan cheese shavings

Preparation time: 10 minutes
Cooking time: 25–35 minutes

1 Heat the oil in a large saucepan. Add the onion and garlic, and cook gently, stirring occasionally, for 5 minutes or until softened but not browned.

2 Add the tomatoes, wine or stock and basil. Cook over a moderate heat for 20–30 minutes or until the sauce is thick.

3 Purée the sauce in a blender or food processor until smooth, then rub it through a fine sieve if a particularly smooth result is required.

4 Add the sugar to balance the acidity of the tomatoes. Stir in salt and pepper to taste and reheat the sauce.

5 Use the sauce as required. Or pour it over freshly cooked pasta, toss well and top with shredded basil and freshly grated or shaved Parmesan cheese.

Some more ideas

• At the beginning of the tomato season, you can boost the flavour of the sauce by adding 1 tbsp tomato purée or sun-dried tomato paste.

• Use 2 cans chopped tomatoes, about 400 g each, with the juice, instead of fresh tomatoes.

Pesto sauce

A little home-made pesto sauce goes a long way as it is packed with flavour. Toss this sauce into piping-hot pasta just before eating. Store any leftover pesto in a screwtop jar in the fridge (cover the surface of the pesto with a little extra oil).

Makes 150 ml (5 fl oz), to serve 4
2 garlic cloves
30 g (1 oz) pine nuts
30 g (1 oz) Parmesan cheese, freshly grated
20 g (¾ oz) fresh basil sprigs
5 tbsp extra virgin olive oil

Preparation time: 10 minutes

1 Place the peeled garlic in a food processor or herb chopper. Add the pine nuts and Parmesan, and process until the ingredients are finely chopped and thoroughly combined.
2 Add the basil, including all the soft stalks. (If the basil is picked from a mature plant with tough stalks, discard these before weighing the sprigs.) Process until the basil is chopped and the mixture begins to clump together.
3 Add the olive oil and process until combined. The sauce should have a fine, slightly grainy texture.

Garlic and herb dressing

Pasta is superb with a simple dressing of garlic, herbs and good olive oil. The secret is to warm the garlic with bay leaves in the oil, to mellow the garlic flavour slightly. Then the dressing should be left to stand for 30 minutes, or longer if possible, so that the flavour of the garlic can infuse the oil.

Serves 4
2 fresh bay leaves
4 garlic cloves, thinly sliced
5 tbsp extra virgin olive oil
grated zest of 1 lemon
4 tbsp snipped fresh chives
4 tbsp chopped fresh parsley
4 tbsp chopped fresh tarragon, sage, marjoram or dill,
    or a mixture of fresh herbs

Preparation time: 10 minutes, plus at least 30 minutes infusing

1 Crease the bay leaves in half and place them in a small saucepan with the garlic. Add about 1 tbsp olive oil and heat gently for 2 minutes or until the oil just begins to sizzle around the garlic. Remove from the heat.
2 Stir in the lemon zest, then pour in the remaining oil. Set aside to infuse for at least 30 minutes.
3 Remove the bay leaves and add the chopped herbs. Toss the dressing into hot pasta and serve.

Béchamel sauce

This classic white sauce is used in a wide variety of dishes. Many flavouring ingredients can be added to make a number of different sauces.

Makes about 600 ml (1 pint), to serve 4

600 ml (1 pint) semi-skimmed milk
1 onion or 2 shallots, halved
1 bay leaf
6 black peppercorns
pinch of grated nutmeg or 1 blade of mace
55 g (2 oz) butter
55 g (2 oz) plain flour
salt and pepper

Preparation time: 5 minutes, plus 10 minutes infusing
Cooking time: 5 minutes

1 Pour the milk into a heavy-based saucepan and add the onion or shallots, bay leaf, peppercorns and nutmeg or mace. Bring just to the boil over a moderate heat, then remove from the heat, cover and set aside to infuse for 10 minutes. Strain the flavoured milk into a jug.

2 Melt the butter in the rinsed-out pan. Stir in the flour and cook gently, stirring occasionally, for 1 minute. Do not allow the flour to brown.

3 Remove the pan from the heat and gradually pour in the milk, stirring or whisking constantly. Return the pan to the heat and bring to the boil, still stirring or whisking.

4 Reduce the heat and simmer the sauce gently for 2 minutes, stirring occasionally, until it is smooth and thick.

5 Taste and add salt and pepper. Serve or use immediately.

Some more ideas

● For a cheese sauce, stir in 55 g (2 oz) grated mature Cheddar, Gruyère or Parmesan cheese and 1 tsp Dijon mustard just before serving.

● For an onion sauce, do not add the onion or shallots when infusing the milk. Finely chop 2 onions and cook in the butter over a low heat for 10 minutes or until softened but not browned, then stir in the flour. Purée the finished sauce in a blender or food processor if a smooth result is required.

● For a mushroom sauce, slice 300 g (10½ oz) button mushrooms and cook in the butter for 5 minutes before stirring in the flour.

● A one-stage béchamel sauce is quick, and it can be a good way of making a lower-fat sauce as the butter can be reduced or omitted. Pour the milk into a heavy-based saucepan and gradually whisk in the flour, sprinkling it lightly over the milk as you whisk. Slice the onion or shallots and add with all the remaining ingredients, including the butter, if using. Whisk the sauce over a moderate heat until it comes to the boil and thickens, then reduce the heat and simmer for 2 minutes. Strain the sauce, or use a draining spoon to remove the flavouring ingredients, and add seasoning to taste.

● For a cornflour-thickened béchamel, omit the butter and flour, and mix 4 tbsp cornflour to a smooth paste with a little of the milk. Infuse the remaining milk as above. Strain and heat to boiling point, then pour a little into the cornflour mixture, stirring. Return this to the milk in the saucepan. Bring to the boil, stirring until the sauce thickens, and simmer for 2 minutes.

fusilli with Parmesan shavings

tagliatelle with olive oil and fresh herbs

spaghetti with lemon juice and black pepper

penne rigati with soft cheese and salmon

Simple and healthy partners for pasta

● Freshly grated or shaved good-quality Parmesan cheese (Parmigiano-Reggiano) is the traditional accompaniment for pasta served with vegetable or meat sauces (cheese does not always go well with fish or shellfish). Parmesan has a lot of flavour, so a little goes a long way, which means it does not over-burden the dish with fat. Pecorino is another sharp and salty cheese that is grated for sprinkling over pasta. Ewe's milk versions of pecorino are particularly useful for people who cannot tolerate cow's milk products.

● Finely chopped or torn fresh herbs, such as basil, parsley, flat-leaf parsley, coriander, chervil, sorrel, oregano, marjoram or thyme, are delicious tossed into pasta dressed with a little olive oil, melted butter or lemon juice and black pepper.
● Lemon juice and black pepper alone make a refreshing and very low-fat dressing for pasta. Add a little freshly grated lemon zest for extra zing.
● Reduced-fat soft white cheese or fromage frais, mixed with flaked poached or canned salmon or chopped fresh herbs, provides a lot of flavour without too much fat.

Pasta First

Good beginnings with tempting pasta

WHY NOT SERVE PASTA as a first course in traditional Italian style? Pasta in soup is always a winner – try tiny pasta shells with cubes of white fish and prawns in a creamy broth, vermicelli in a provençal vegetable soup flavoured with aromatic pesto, or fine rice noodles in a spicy beef broth inspired by the cooking of South-east Asia. On chilly days, enjoy pasta shapes in a vitamin-rich blend of leafy greens. Pasta lends itself to imaginative starters, such as lasagne sheets enclosing delicate spinach and salmon creams to be served with a fresh herb sauce. And tasty dim sum dumplings, in their pasta wrappers, will get a Chinese meal off to a grand start.

Sea bass and fennel soup

This colourful soup is light yet satisfying. Chunky cubes of white fish, prawns and small pasta shells combine with the full flavours of fennel and leek to make a delicious first course. Serve with warm crusty bread, or chunky slices off a hearty mixed-grain loaf or poppy-seed bread plait.

Serves 6

2 tbsp extra virgin olive oil

1 leek, sliced

1 bulb of fennel, roughly chopped

300 ml (10 fl oz) dry white wine

900 ml (1½ pints) fish stock

125 g (4½ oz) conchigliette (soup pasta shells)

450 g (1 lb) sea bass fillets, skinned and cut into chunks

2 tomatoes, skinned, seeded and chopped

1 tbsp cornflour

115 g (4 oz) peeled cooked prawns

½ tsp chilli sauce, or to taste

2 tbsp single cream

2 tbsp chopped fresh parsley

salt and pepper

Preparation time: 15 minutes

Cooking time: 20 minutes

1 Heat the oil in a large heavy-based saucepan. Add the leek and fennel, and cook for about 5 minutes, stirring occasionally.

2 Pour in the wine and fish stock, and bring to the boil. Add the pasta and stir the soup once, then leave to simmer for about 8 minutes or until the pasta is almost tender.

3 Gently stir in the chunks of sea bass and the tomatoes, with salt and pepper to taste. Cook over a low heat for a further 2–3 minutes or until the fish is just firm.

4 Meanwhile, blend the cornflour to a smooth paste with 2 tbsp water. Stir the cornflour mixture into the soup and bring it to the boil, stirring constantly. Add the cooked prawns and simmer gently for a further minute.

5 Stir in the chilli sauce to taste. Add the cream and parsley, stir to mix and serve immediately.

Some more ideas

● Different types and brands of chilli sauce vary widely in flavour and some are very hot, so start with just a dash if you are not familiar with the product and then add more to taste.

● Use 450 g (1 lb) each of monkfish fillet and scrubbed mussels instead of sea bass and prawns; add the mussels with the fish. Replace the fennel with 4 sliced celery sticks and 2 diced carrots. Discard any unopened mussels at the end of cooking.

● Plain low-fat yogurt can be added instead of cream, but do not heat the soup once the yogurt has been added or it will separate.

● Omit the chilli sauce and instead add 2 tbsp dry white vermouth; use chopped fresh dill instead of parsley.

Plus points

● White fish is a rich source of protein and it contains very little fat. It is also a good source of vitamin B_{12}, which is essential for the formation of red blood cells and for maintaining a healthy nervous system.

● Bulb or Florence fennel contains more phytoestrogen than most vegetables. This naturally occurring plant hormone encourages the body to excrete excess oestrogen, a high level of which is linked with a greater risk of breast cancer.

Each serving provides

kcal 263, **protein** 21 g, **fat** 7 g (of which saturated fat 1.5 g), **carbohydrate** 20 g (of which sugars 2.5 g), **fibre** 2 g

✓✓✓	B_1, B_6, B_{12}, E, niacin
✓✓	C, copper, iron, selenium
✓	potassium

pasta first

Old-fashioned chicken noodle soup

Much of this soup's appeal is in its simplicity. Packed with fresh flavours, mixing pasta with bites of chicken and a bounty of just-tender vegetables, it is easy to see why this soup is traditionally eaten as a restorative. Serve it as a starter and enjoy the extra chicken in sandwiches the next day.

Serves 4

125 g (4½ oz) spaghetti or linguine, broken
    into 5 cm (2 in) pieces

1 carrot, halved lengthways and thinly sliced

1 celery stick, thinly sliced

55 g (2 oz) small broccoli florets

1 can sweetcorn in water, about 200 g,
    drained

2 tbsp finely chopped fresh parsley

2 tsp fresh thyme leaves

Chicken broth

1 chicken, about 1.35 kg (3 lb), skinned and
    jointed, or 4 chicken quarters, skinned

2 onions, halved, the inner layer of skin
    left on

3 carrots, chopped

3 celery sticks, chopped

1 bouquet garni

4 black peppercorns

salt and pepper

Preparation time: about 45 minutes
Cooking time: 1¼ hours

Each serving provides

kcal 275, **protein** 19 g, **fat** 4.5 g (of which
saturated fat 1 g), **carbohydrate** 41 g (of
which sugars 9 g), **fibre** 5 g

✓✓✓	A, B$_1$, B$_6$, E, niacin
✓✓	C, folate, iron
✓	zinc

1 First make the broth. Put the chicken joints in a large, heavy-based stockpot or saucepan. Add the onions, carrots and celery, then pour in about 2 litres (3½ pints) cold water to cover the ingredients. Bring to the boil, skimming the surface constantly until all grey scum is removed.

2 Reduce the heat to low immediately the liquid boils. Add the bouquet garni, peppercorns and 1 tsp salt. Partially cover the pan and simmer for 1 hour, skimming as necessary. Test the chicken joints after 30–40 minutes; remove them as soon as the juices run clear when the joints are pierced with the point of a knife. Set aside.

3 Line a large colander or sieve with dampened muslin and place it over a large heatproof bowl, then strain the broth through this. Discard the vegetables and flavouring ingredients. Return 1.5 litres (2¾ pints) of broth to the rinsed-out pan. Skim off any excess fat on the surface of the broth. Cool and freeze the leftover broth to use as a chicken stock in other recipes.

4 When the chicken is cool enough to handle, remove and discard all the bones. Cut 225 g (8 oz) meat into bite-sized pieces for use in the soup. Reserve the remaining chicken for sandwiches or other recipes.

5 Bring the broth to the boil, then reduce the heat so the broth is simmering. Add the spaghetti or linguine and the carrot, and simmer for 4 minutes. Add the celery, broccoli and sweetcorn, and continue cooking for about 5 minutes or until the pasta and all the vegetables are just tender.

6 Stir in the chicken with seasoning to taste and heat through. Sprinkle in the parsley and thyme, and serve the soup at once.

Plus points

• Unlike the majority of vegetables, which are most nutritious when eaten raw, carrots are a better source of beta-carotene when they are cooked. Cooking breaks down their cell membranes, making it easier for the body to convert the beta-carotene they contain into vitamin A.

• Both the dark and white chicken meat can be added to the soup. The dark meat contains twice as much iron and zinc as the light meat.

• Chicken is an excellent source of protein and it provides many of the B vitamins, particularly B$_1$ and niacin.

Some more ideas

- Add 450 g (1 lb) of the cooked chicken to the soup if you are serving it as a light lunch or supper rather than a starter.
- Replace the chicken with two 600 g (1 lb 5 oz) turkey drumsticks.

- Increase the fibre content by using wholemeal instead of white spaghetti. Alternatively, add 1 can butter beans, about 400 g, drained and rinsed. Stir in the beans with the chicken and just heat through.
- Vary the vegetables to suit the season –

small cauliflower florets, finely diced celeriac, sliced mushrooms or diced green, red and yellow peppers are all ideal.
- Thicker fettuccine or tagliatelle, or even small pasta shapes, can be used instead of the spaghetti or linguine.

Vietnamese broth with noodles

Punchy flavours and aromatic ingredients transform a light broth into an exotic dish that makes a substantial starter or a light meal. The ingredients are not fried before being simmered – making this a great low-fat soup – so select prime-quality lean steak which tastes excellent when poached.

Serves 2

25 g (scant 1 oz) dried shiitake mushrooms

75 g (2½ oz) fine rice noodles, such as
   vermicelli

170 g (6 oz) lean rump steak, diced

500 ml (17 fl oz) beef stock

2 tbsp fish sauce

1 heaped tsp grated fresh root ginger

30 g (1 oz) bean sprouts

½ small onion, thinly sliced

2 spring onions, thinly sliced

2 small fresh red bird's eye chillies or
   1 medium red chilli, seeded and finely
   chopped

1 tbsp shredded fresh mint

1 tbsp shredded fresh coriander

1 tbsp shredded fresh basil

To serve

lime wedges

soy sauce (optional)

Preparation time: 20 minutes, plus 20 minutes
   soaking

Cooking time: 10–15 minutes

Each serving provides
kcal 300, **protein** 23 g, **fat** 4 g (of which
saturated fat 1.5 g), **carbohydrate** 42 g (of
which sugars 2 g), **fibre** 0.8 g

✓✓✓ B$_1$, B$_6$, B$_{12}$, E, niacin

✓✓   iron, zinc

---

1 Rinse the shiitake mushrooms and put them in a small bowl. Place the rice noodles in a large bowl. Cover the mushrooms with boiling water and leave to soak for 20 minutes. Cover the rice noodles with boiling water and soak for 4 minutes, or according to the packet instructions. Drain the noodles and set aside until they are needed.

2 Drain the mushrooms and pour the soaking liquid into a large saucepan. Trim off and discard any tough stalks from the mushrooms, then slice them and add to the pan with the diced steak, stock, fish sauce and ginger. Bring to the boil, then simmer for 10–15 minutes or until the steak is cooked and tender. Skim off any scum that rises to the surface of the soup during cooking.

3 Divide the noodles, bean sprouts and sliced onion between 2 large, deep soup bowls. Use a draining spoon to remove the steak and mushrooms from the broth and divide them between the bowls. Ladle the broth into the bowls, then scatter the spring onions, chillies, mint, coriander and basil over the top.

4 Serve immediately, with the lime wedges – the juice can be squeezed into the broth to taste. Soy sauce can also be added, if liked.

Plus points

- In common with other red meats, beef is a good source of iron and zinc, and the iron in meat is far more easily absorbed by the body than iron from vegetable sources.
- Beef is now far leaner than it used to be, and well-trimmed lean cuts can contain as little as 4% fat.

Some more ideas

- For a vegetarian version of this soup, use tofu and vegetable stock instead of beef and beef stock, and soy sauce or dry sherry instead of the fish sauce. Cook the tofu gently for only 2 minutes or until heated through.
- The bean sprouts can be replaced by shavings of carrot and chopped celery. Vary the quantities of spring onion, chilli and fresh herbs to taste.
- Any thin Oriental noodles can be used in place of rice noodles, including the readily available Chinese egg noodles. Cook or soak the chosen noodles according to the packet instructions.
- For a warm, spicy flavour, add a good pinch of ground cinnamon with the ginger.

Chickpea soup with orzo and asparagus

This filling soup is easy to make, tasty and virtually fat-free. Offer crusty bread as an accompaniment.

For a main meal, serve with a little strong-flavoured cheese, which tastes very good with the soup.

Serves 4

1 can chickpeas, about 400 g, drained

1 onion, coarsely chopped

2 garlic cloves, chopped

1 litre (1¾ pints) vegetable or chicken stock

150 g (5½ oz) asparagus, trimmed and cut into bite-sized pieces

170 g (6 oz) orzo (rice-shaped pasta) or other soup pasta

salt and pepper

To garnish

fine strips of zest from 1 lemon

2 tbsp chopped fresh parsley, preferably flat-leaf

1 lemon, cut into wedges, to serve

Preparation time: 15 minutes

Cooking time: about 40 minutes

Each serving provides Ⓥ

kcal 290, **protein** 14 g, **fat** 4 g (of which saturated fat 0.5 g), **carbohydrate** 52 g (of which sugars 3.5 g), **fibre** 6.5 g

✓✓✓	B₁, E, niacin
✓✓	B₆, folate
✓	copper, iron

1 Put the chickpeas, onion, garlic and stock in a saucepan and bring to the boil. Reduce the heat and simmer for about 20 minutes or until the onion is very tender and the chickpeas are falling apart. If the mixture is becoming too thick, add a little more stock or water.

2 Ladle about one-third of the soup into a blender or food processor and purée it until it is smooth. Return the puréed soup to the pan and bring back to simmering point. Add the asparagus, cover the pan and cook gently for 5–6 minutes or until the asparagus is just tender.

3 Meanwhile, cook the orzo or other pasta shapes in boiling water for 10–12 minutes, or according to the packet instructions, until al dente. Drain the pasta and add it to the soup with seasoning to taste.

4 Mix together the lemon zest and parsley for the garnish. Top each bowl of soup with a small spoonful of the lemon and parsley garnish, and serve immediately, offering lemon wedges so that the juice can be added to the soup to taste.

Some more ideas

• Use small broccoli florets instead of asparagus. Broccoli is an excellent source of vitamin C and the quantity in this soup will provide about one-quarter of the recommended daily intake of that vital vitamin.

• There are many tiny pasta shapes for soup (called *pastina* in Italy). Orzo is rice-shaped; other shapes are stelline (stars), ditalini (tubes), conchigliette (shells) and farfallini (bow ties). You can also use larger pasta shapes (penne or rigatoni, for example), if you prefer.

• For a spicier soup, season with cayenne instead of black pepper, or add a few drops of Tabasco sauce.

Plus points

• Chickpeas, along with other pulses, are a good source of dietary fibre, particularly the soluble fibre that can help to reduce high blood cholesterol levels.

• Asparagus is a rich source of many of the B vitamins, especially folate. A good intake of folate is important during the early stages of pregnancy, to prevent birth defects such as spina bifida. New research suggests that folate may also have a role in helping to prevent Alzheimer's disease.

Vegetable soup with fragrant pesto

This soup is based on pistou, the classic French soup from Provence. Laden with vegetables and pasta, and flavoured with pesto, the delicious basil and Parmesan sauce, it makes a fabulous change from minestrone, its Italian counterpart. French bread is the traditional accompaniment, plus a glass of wine.

Serves 4

1 tbsp extra virgin olive oil

1 leek, thinly sliced

1 large courgette, diced

150 g (5½ oz) French beans, cut into short lengths

2 garlic cloves, crushed

1.3 litres (2¼ pints) vegetable stock

250 g (9 oz) tomatoes, chopped

85 g (3 oz) vermicelli, broken into small pieces

2 tbsp pesto sauce

pepper

To serve (optional)

4 tbsp freshly grated Parmesan cheese

Preparation time: 10 minutes

Cooking time: about 30 minutes

1 Heat the oil in a large saucepan. Add the leek, courgette, beans and garlic and fry over a moderately high heat for about 5 minutes or until the vegetables are softened and beginning to turn brown.

2 Pour in the vegetable stock. Stir in the tomatoes and add freshly ground black pepper to taste. Bring to the boil, then reduce the heat and cover the pan. Simmer over a low heat for 10 minutes or until the vegetables are tender, but still holding their shape.

3 Stir in the vermicelli. Cover the pan again and simmer for a further 5 minutes or until the pasta is al dente.

4 Ladle the soup into bowls and add 1½ tsp pesto to each. Stir, then serve, offering the Parmesan cheese separately to stir into the soup.

Plus points

● Tomatoes contain lycopene, a carotenoid compound that acts as an antioxidant. Recent studies suggest that lycopene may help to protect against bladder and pancreatic cancers.

● All cheeses are a good source of calcium, and they contain vitamins A and D. Vitamin D is fat-soluble, so the more fat in the cheese, the more vitamin D it provides. Parmesan is a high-fat cheese, so adding the optional spoonful to your bowl of soup will increase the fat content, but will also increase the calcium and vitamins.

Some more ideas

● For a more substantial soup, or to increase the protein content for a vegetarian meal, stir in 1 can cannellini or flageolet beans, about 400 g, well drained. Add an extra 150 ml (5 fl oz) stock and increase the pesto in each serving to 2 tsp.

● When fresh tomatoes are not available, use 1 can chopped tomatoes, about 400 g, well drained, instead.

● Use quick-cook macaroni instead of vermicelli.

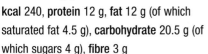

Each serving provides

kcal 240, **protein** 12 g, **fat** 12 g (of which saturated fat 4.5 g), **carbohydrate** 20.5 g (of which sugars 4 g), **fibre** 3 g

✓✓✓ B₁, B₆, E, niacin

✓✓ calcium

✓ C, folate, iron

pasta first

Soup of leafy greens and herbs

Not only is this soup delicious, you can almost feel those vitamin-packed leafy greens doing you good as you eat it. Hearty but not too heavy, it is a wonderful dish for summer and autumn. You can use all sorts of greens – simply adjust the cooking time accordingly.

Serves 4

2 tbsp extra virgin olive oil

1 leek, white part only, cut into thin strips

1 small onion, chopped

½ carrot, thinly sliced

4 garlic cloves, chopped

½ tsp fennel seeds

2 tbsp chopped fresh parsley

2 slices Parma ham, about 55 g (2 oz) in total, trimmed of fat, then cut into thin strips or chopped

150 g (5½ oz) Swiss chard, spinach or spring greens, or a mixture, very finely shredded

3 small ripe tomatoes or whole canned tomatoes, diced

1.5 litres (2¾ pints) chicken or vegetable stock

pinch of crushed dried red chillies (optional)

250 g (9 oz) small pasta shapes, such as conchigliette (shells) or ditalini (small thimbles)

salt and pepper

To serve

55 g (2 oz) fresh basil, stalks discarded, then thinly sliced or torn

4 tbsp freshly grated Parmesan cheese

4 tbsp chopped young rocket (optional)

Preparation time: 20–25 minutes

Cooking time: about 30 minutes

1 Heat the oil in a large saucepan. Add the leek and onion and cook for 5 minutes or until slightly softened. Add the carrot, garlic, fennel seeds, parsley and Parma ham. Continue cooking for about 5 minutes, stirring occasionally.

2 Stir in the shredded greens and the tomatoes, and cover the pan. Cook for about 2 minutes or until the greens are slightly softened, then pour in the stock. Add the crushed dried chillies, if using. Season to taste with salt and pepper. Bring to the boil, then simmer over a moderately high heat for about 5 minutes or until the shredded greens are just tender.

3 Meanwhile, cook the pasta in boiling water for 10–12 minutes, or according to the packet instructions, until al dente. Drain well.

4 Divide the pasta among 4 serving bowls. Ladle the soup into the bowls and sprinkle with the basil, grated Parmesan and rocket, if using. Serve immediately.

Some more ideas

• Other greens that are good in this soup include Chinese leaves, pak choy, Chinese choy sum, kale and watercress. Coarser leaves, such as kale, will take a little more time to cook than tender leaves like watercress.

• For a vegetarian soup with a Middle Eastern flavour, omit the Parma ham and use vegetable stock. Stir 150 g (5½ oz) plain low-fat yogurt until smooth, then stir into the soup, off the heat. Add 3 tbsp chopped fresh coriander and the juice of ½ lemon (or to taste). Serve sprinkled with paprika and cayenne pepper to taste.

• For a Chinese-style version, omit the fennel seeds, parsley, Parma ham, basil and Parmesan, and spice the soup with 1–2 tbsp peeled and finely chopped fresh root ginger and soy sauce to taste. Add 100 g (3½ oz) firm tofu, cut into small cubes.

Plus points

• Dark green, leafy vegetables, such as Swiss chard, spinach and spring greens, provide good amounts of the antioxidants vitamin C and beta-carotene, as well as the B vitamins niacin, folate and B_6.

Each serving provides

kcal 405, protein 19 g, fat 13 g (of which saturated fat 4 g), carbohydrate 54 g (of which sugars 5.5 g), fibre 3 g

✓✓✓	A, B_1, B_6, E, niacin
✓✓	C, folate, calcium, iron
✓	copper

pasta first

Spinach and salmon timbales

Ideal for a dinner party first course, these attractive timbales are surprisingly easy to make. Layers of spinach and lasagne enclose a creamy filling of ricotta cheese and fresh salmon, and the timbales are served with a fresh herb sauce. Crisp Melba toast will complement the tender texture.

Serves 4

5 sheets fresh lasagne, about 100 g (3½ oz)
   in total (see page 19 for home-made pasta)
250 g (9 oz) spinach, trimmed
115 g (4 oz) ricotta cheese
1 egg, beaten
a little grated nutmeg
170 g (6 oz) salmon fillet, skinned
2 tsp chopped fresh fennel or dill
grated zest of ½ lime
salt and pepper
fresh fennel or dill to garnish (optional)

Herb sauce

15 g (½ oz) butter
1 tbsp plain flour
200 ml (7 fl oz) semi-skimmed milk
2 tsp lime juice
3 tbsp chopped mixed fresh chives, parsley,
   thyme and marjoram
2 tbsp single cream

Preparation time: 50 minutes
Cooking time: 20 minutes

Each serving provides

kcal 300, **protein** 19 g, **fat** 16 g (of which saturated fat 7 g), **carbohydrate** 21 g (of which sugars 5 g), **fibre** 2 g

✓✓✓	A, B₁, B₆, B₁₂, E, niacin
✓✓	C, folate
✓	calcium, iron

1 Preheat the oven to 200ºC (400ºF, gas mark 6). Cook the lasagne in boiling water for 3–5 minutes, or according to the packet instructions, until al dente. Drain and rinse under cold water. Drain on a clean tea-towel, in a single layer, then cut each sheet of lasagne in half lengthways.

2 Rinse the spinach and place in a large saucepan. Cover and cook over a moderately high heat for 2–3 minutes (the water clinging to the leaves will provide enough moisture). Shake the pan occasionally so that the spinach cooks evenly. Drain well. Use 4 large leaves to line 4 lightly oiled 175 ml (6 fl oz) ramekin dishes. Chop the remaining spinach and set aside.

3 Lay 2 lasagne strips in each spinach-lined ramekin, overlapping them in a cross shape. Leave excess pasta hanging over the edge.

4 Mix half the ricotta cheese with the chopped spinach. Add half of the beaten egg, the nutmeg and seasoning to taste, and mix thoroughly.

5 Cut the salmon into 1 cm (½ in) dice and mix with the remaining ricotta cheese and beaten egg. Stir in the fennel or dill, grated lime zest and seasoning to taste until thoroughly combined. Divide the salmon mixture evenly among the ramekins.

6 Cut the remaining 2 strips of pasta across in half and lay a piece in each ramekin, pressing it in neatly on top of the salmon mixture. Spoon the spinach mixture into the dishes and fold the overhanging pasta strips over the top. Cut out 4 pieces of foil and brush them lightly with oil, then use them to cover the ramekin dishes. Place in the oven and bake for 20 minutes.

7 Meanwhile, make the herb sauce. Melt the butter in a small saucepan. Stir in the flour, then gradually stir in the milk and bring to the boil, stirring constantly. Stir in the lime juice, herbs, cream and seasoning to taste. Remove from the heat.

8 Run a flat-bladed knife around the edges of the dishes to loosen the timbales. Cover each one with a plate, invert and lift off the dish. Pour the herb sauce around, garnish with fennel or dill, if using, and serve.

Plus points

● Spinach provides good amounts of several antioxidants, including vitamins C and E. It also offers carotenoid compounds and substantial amounts of B vitamins, including folate, niacin and B₆.

Some more ideas

● For a light lunch, serve the timbales with a generous side salad of cucumber and watercress and additional pasta. Cut a further 8 sheets of lasagne into fine strips. Cut 1 large carrot and 1 large leek into fine strips. Cook the shredded pasta and vegetables together in boiling water for about 5 minutes or until tender. Drain and serve hot.

● If you do not have ramekin dishes, layer the sheets of lasagne and the spinach and salmon mixtures in one large container, such as a soufflé dish (do not line the dish with spinach leaves; chop all the spinach and use in the filling). Bake for an extra 10 minutes.

Cheese-baked peppers with linguine

These stuffed peppers, filled with thin noodles in a savoury custard, make an ideal first course to serve 4, or a light vegetarian lunch for 2 served with an assortment of salads and plenty of warm bread. Any colour of pepper suggested can be used, but avoid green peppers which are not as sweet.

Serves 4

2 large red, orange or yellow peppers

45 g (1½ oz) linguine

2 eggs, beaten

55 g (2 oz) mature Cheddar cheese, grated

1¼ tsp English mustard powder

3 tbsp semi-skimmed milk

3 tbsp snipped fresh chives

¼ tsp dried marjoram or oregano

2 tomatoes, skinned, seeded and diced

salt and pepper

fresh whole chives to garnish

To serve (optional)

salad leaves

Preparation time: about 40 minutes

Cooking time: 20–25 minutes

1 Preheat the oven to 180°C (350°F, gas mark 4). Halve the peppers lengthways, carefully cutting through the stalk. Remove the pith and seeds. Cook the pepper shells in boiling water for 6–8 minutes or until tender. Drain thoroughly and place on kitchen paper.

2 Cook the linguine in boiling water for 10 minutes, or according to the packet instructions, until al dente. Drain well and set aside.

3 Beat the eggs with the cheese, mustard, milk, chives and marjoram or oregano. Stir in the tomatoes and seasoning to taste.

4 Place the peppers in a shallow ovenproof dish or roasting tin, supporting them with pieces of crumpled foil, if necessary, to ensure that they are level (otherwise the filling will spill out). Half fill each pepper with linguine, then spoon the egg and cheese mixture over the pasta.

5 Bake for 20–25 minutes or until the filling is set and beginning to turn golden. Serve garnished with whole chives, with an accompaniment of mixed salad leaves, if liked.

Plus points

• Peppers are an excellent source of vitamin C. Weight for weight, they contain more than twice as much vitamin C as oranges. Red, orange and yellow peppers are also rich in beta-carotene. Vitamin C and beta-carotene are powerful antioxidants that can help to protect against many diseases, including cancer and heart disease.

Some more ideas

• Use 55 g (2 oz) fresh linguine instead of dried. Fresh linguine will only need to be cooked for 2–3 minutes.

• For a more substantial dish, cook an additional 140 g (5 oz) linguine while the peppers are baking and toss it with 1 tbsp snipped fresh chives. Serve this pasta as a base for the peppers.

• To make a tasty supper for 2, thoroughly drain and flake 1 can tuna fish in brine, about 100 g, and add it to the egg mixture. Serve 2 pepper halves per person.

• Stir 4 stoned green olives, finely chopped, into the egg mixture.

Each serving provides

kcal 180, **protein** 10 g, **fat** 9 g (of which saturated fat 4 g), **carbohydrate** 15 g (of which sugars 7 g), **fibre** 2 g

✓✓✓ A, B₁, B₆, C, E, niacin

✓✓ B₁₂

Dressed noodles

Less is definitely more with this robustly flavoured, low-fat pasta sauce that just lightly coats the noodles in traditional Italian style. The noodles make a satisfying carbohydrate-packed starter that will serve 6 before a light main course, or a simple meal for 4 with a crunchy salad and fruit to follow.

Serves 6

2 tbsp extra virgin olive oil

1 large garlic clove, crushed

4 shallots, about 85 g (3 oz) in total, finely chopped

1 can chopped tomatoes, about 400 g

240 ml (8 fl oz) red wine

1 bay leaf

2 sprigs of fresh rosemary

2 strips of lemon zest

½ tsp sugar

400 g (14 oz) spinach tagliatelle

2 tbsp single cream (optional)

salt and pepper

To garnish

30 g (1 oz) stoned black olives, quartered

fresh basil leaves, torn

4 tbsp freshly grated Parmesan cheese (optional)

Preparation time: 15 minutes

Cooking time: about 1 hour

Each serving provides

kcal 315, **protein** 8.5 g, **fat** 5 g (of which saturated fat 1 g), **carbohydrate** 54 g (of which sugars 4.5 g), **fibre** 3 g

✓✓	A, calcium
✓	C, E, niacin, copper

1 Heat the olive oil in a large heavy-based saucepan over a moderate heat. Add the garlic and shallots, and cook for about 3 minutes, stirring frequently, until the shallots are soft.

2 Stir in the tomatoes with their juice, the wine, bay leaf, rosemary, lemon zest and sugar. Bring to the boil, then reduce the heat and partially cover the pan. Simmer for 45 minutes, stirring occasionally, until the sauce is reduced and thick, with only a small amount of liquid on the surface.

3 Allow to cool for a few minutes, then discard the bay leaf and rosemary. Purée the sauce, including the lemon zest, in a blender or food processor. Press the sauce through a fine sieve into the rinsed-out saucepan. Bring back to the boil, then leave to simmer very gently while you cook the pasta.

4 Cook the pasta in boiling water for 10–12 minutes, or according to the packet instructions, until al dente. Drain, reserving a few spoonfuls of the cooking liquid.

5 Add the cream to the sauce, if using, with seasoning to taste. Stir in the noodles until they are all coated with the sauce. If the sauce is too thick to coat the pasta, thin it with the reserved cooking liquid.

6 Transfer the noodles to a serving dish. Sprinkle with the olives, basil and Parmesan, if using, and serve.

Some more ideas

● Make Italian-style vongole or clam sauce by adding 1 can clams, about 300 g, well drained, to the sauce at the end of step 3. Use sprigs of fresh parsley instead of rosemary. The clams, a good low-fat source of iron, should not be boiled or they will become tough, so simmer the sauce very gently while you cook the pasta.

● Boost the dietary fibre by using wholemeal tagliatelle or other noodles.

● For a more substantial sauce, without increasing the fat, add fresh vegetables cut into bite-sized pieces in step 3 and simmer until they are just tender but still crisp.

Plus points

● Lycopene, the natural pigment that gives tomatoes their colour, can reduce the risk of heart disease and prostate cancer. A 6-year study at Harvard medical school found that eating tomato products more than twice a week was associated with a reduced risk of prostate cancer of up to 34%. Processed tomatoes (canned or tomato purée) contain higher concentrations of lycopene than fresh tomatoes.

Dim sum with dipping sauce

These Chinese dumplings, known as shao may *or* shiu may, *have a chicken filling, which is lighter than the traditional pork mixture. Wonton wrappers, sold in Oriental food stores, can be used, or you can make your own pasta wrapping. Serve these dim sum as the starter for a multi-course Chinese meal.*

Makes 50, to serve 6

1 can water chestnuts, about 200 g, drained and chopped
4 spring onions, thinly sliced
2 tbsp chopped fresh coriander
1 tbsp dark soy sauce
1 tbsp toasted sesame oil
340 g (12 oz) minced chicken
1 tsp caster sugar
1 tbsp finely chopped fresh root ginger
5 garlic cloves, finely chopped
30 g (1 oz) fresh shiitake mushrooms, chopped
1 tbsp cornflour, plus extra for dusting
50 wonton wrappers
150 g (5½ oz) kale, Swiss chard or spring greens
salt and cayenne pepper

Dipping sauce

hoisin sauce, chopped spring onions, chopped fresh coriander, soy sauce and/or toasted sesame oil

Preparation time: 45 minutes
Cooking time: 8–10 minutes per batch

Each serving provides

kcal 150, **protein** 14 g, **fat** 5 g (of which saturated fat 1 g), **carbohydrate** 13 g (of which sugars 3 g), **fibre** 1 g

✓ A, niacin

1 Mix together the water chestnuts, spring onions, coriander, soy sauce and sesame oil. Add the chicken, sugar, ginger, garlic and shiitake mushrooms. Stir in the cornflour with salt and cayenne pepper to taste, and mix well. Cook a small spoonful of the chicken mixture in a frying pan, then taste it to check the seasoning.

2 Dust a plate with cornflour. Place about 1 tsp filling on the middle of a wonton wrapper. Dampen the wrapper slightly just around the filling. Gather up the wrapper, pinching it around the filling to form a cup, open at the top and with 'frilly' edges. Set aside on the plate, and fill the remaining wrappers.

3 Line a multi-layered steamer with kale, Swiss chard or spring greens. Stand the dim sum on the leaves and steam over rapidly boiling water for 8–10 minutes. Serve hot, with the ingredients for the dipping sauce in individual bowls so that each diner can mix them together to make a sauce to their own taste.

Some more ideas

● Make your own dough to enclose the dim sum: the wrappers will be slightly thicker and not frilly around the top edge, but they are equally delicious. Mix 200 g (7 oz) strong plain flour with a pinch of salt in a bowl. Make a well

in the centre and add 1 tbsp sunflower oil and 4 tbsp boiling water. Mix well. Cover with cling film and set aside to rest for 15 minutes. Then knead the dough until smooth, roll into a sausage shape and cut into 10 equal pieces. Each piece of dough is enough to make 5 dim sum. Cut one piece into 5 portions, leaving the others covered to prevent them from drying out. Roll out one of the small pieces of dough into a 5 cm (2 in) circle. Place about 1 tsp of the filling in the centre of the dough. Pinch the dough up to form a cup around the filling, leaving it open at the top. Place on a cornflour-dusted plate, and repeat with the remaining filling and dough. Steam as for dim sum in wonton wrappers.

● Use 3 dried shiitake mushrooms, soaked until pliable, then drained and chopped, instead of fresh shiitake.

● For a vegetarian filling, mix 10 fresh shiitake mushrooms, chopped, with 225 g (8 oz) mashed tofu and 3 finely chopped garlic cloves.

Plus points

● Garlic, onions, leeks and chives contain allicin which has anti-fungal and antibiotic properties. Garlic also contains other compounds that have been shown in animal studies to inactivate carcinogens and suppress the growth of tumours.

For Maximum Vitality

Satisfying salads full of all good things

PASTA MAKES A SPLENDID BASE for healthy salads, blending well with just about any ingredient you can think of. For a summer lunch or supper dish, nothing beats a Mediterranean-style salad of linguine and freshly poached seafood, or saffron couscous with garlicky vegetables. Snail-shaped lumache in herby yogurt and tomato dressing is another delicious option, or try a creamy salad of pasta spirals, turkey, grapes and pecans. For a lighter touch, toss together a zesty salad of penne, oranges and bean sprouts, an ideal side dish.

Mediterranean seafood salad

Poached mussels, prawns and scallops bring the flavour of southern Italy to this chilled salad. Black squid-ink pasta would be served in restaurants along the Amalfi coast, but spinach, red pepper and egg linguine are also suitable. Enjoy this as a tempting summer lunch or supper dish.

Serves 4

2 red peppers, quartered and seeded

225 g (8 oz) raw king or tiger prawns, peeled

500 g (1 lb 2 oz) mussels in shells, scrubbed

125 g (4½ oz) scallops, preferably small
   bay scallops or queens

200 g (7 oz) linguine, preferably black
   squid-ink linguine

1 tbsp capers in brine, rinsed

salt and pepper

Poaching liquid

1 fresh red chilli (optional)

1 garlic clove

240 ml (8 fl oz) dry white wine

1 bay leaf

1 lemon, thinly sliced

1 shallot, thinly sliced

Dressing

4 tbsp extra virgin olive oil

1½ tbsp lemon juice

To serve

1 head radicchio

2 tbsp finely chopped fresh parsley

1 lemon, cut into wedges

Preparation time: about 1 hour, plus cooling, at
   least 1 hour chilling and 30 minutes
   standing before serving

1 First prepare the poaching liquid. If using the chilli, spear it on a wooden cocktail stick with the garlic. Alternatively, if not using the chilli, slice the garlic. Place in a large heavy-based saucepan with the wine, bay leaf, lemon, shallot and ½ tsp salt. Pour in 120 ml (4 fl oz) water. Bring to the boil, then remove from the heat, cover and leave to infuse while you prepare the other ingredients. Taste the liquid occasionally and remove the chilli at any point if its flavour is strong enough in the liquid for your taste.

2 Preheat the grill to high. Grill the peppers, skin side up, for about 10 minutes or until blistered and blackened. Place in a polythene bag and leave to cool for 5 minutes. Peel off the skins, then finely dice the flesh.

3 Whisk the dressing ingredients together in a large bowl. Season and set aside. Cut a slit along the back of each prawn, and remove and discard the black vein, if necessary. Set aside.

4 To prepare the mussels, discard any broken ones or open ones that do not close when tapped. Bring the poaching liquid back to the boil, then reduce the heat to low. Add the mussels and cook for 2–3 minutes or until the shells are open. Using a draining spoon, transfer the mussels to a bowl. Discard any mussels that are still closed. Remove and discard the shells. Add the mussels to the dressing.

5 Poach the prawns in the same liquid for 2 minutes or until they turn from bluey-grey to pink. Remove the prawns with a draining spoon and add to the mussels in the dressing.

6 Poach the scallops for 1½ minutes or until they turn opaque. Remove with a draining spoon. Remove any red corals, and chop or discard them as preferred. Chop large scallops, then add to the mussels and prawns.

7 Strain the poaching liquid, then return it to the pan and add water so there is enough to cook the pasta. Bring to the boil. Add the pasta and cook for 10 minutes, or according to the packet instructions, until al dente. Drain well, then add to the seafood mixture with the diced red peppers and toss well. Leave to cool completely, then cover and chill for at least 1 hour.

8 Remove the salad from the fridge 30 minutes before serving. Add the capers and seasoning to taste, and toss the salad lightly. Line a serving bowl or platter with radicchio leaves and pile the salad on top. Sprinkle with the chopped parsley and serve at once, with lemon wedges for squeezing over each portion to taste.

Plus points

● Shellfish are a good source of protein, both low in fat and calories. They contain useful amounts of many B vitamins, particularly B_{12}. They are also a good source of the antioxidant selenium. Although shellfish contain high levels of cholesterol, it is not easily absorbed, and some studies suggest that eating shellfish can help to lower, not raise, blood cholesterol levels.

Some more ideas

● Use 125 g (4½ oz) shelled cooked mussels, thawed if frozen, instead of fresh mussels.

● Replace the mussels or scallops with 1 can tuna fish in brine, about 200 g, well drained. Like all oily fish, tuna is a good source of vitamin D, which the body uses to maintain calcium levels in the blood.

● To increase the iron content, replace the scallops with clams, which contain at least three times as much iron. Cook the clams until their shells open, then remove them from the shells and add to the dressing.

Each serving provides

kcal 415, **protein** 29 g, **fat** 14 g (of which saturated fat 2 g), **carbohydrate** 46 g (of which sugars 6.5 g), **fibre** 3 g

✓✓✓ A, B_{12}, C, copper

✓✓ E, niacin, iron, selenium

Piquant pasta and tuna salad

The dressing for this simple, colourful salad has a sweet-sour flavour, which perfectly complements the lightly cooked courgette, tuna, tomatoes and al dente pasta. Serve the salad cool, but not chilled, or try it while it is still warm. Mini pitta bread is good served alongside, to mop up the dressing.

Serves 4

250 g (9 oz) pasta twists or spirals, such as cavatappi, fusilli or rotini, or other shapes

2 tbsp extra virgin olive oil

1 onion, chopped

1 garlic clove, chopped

2 courgettes, thinly sliced

2 tsp caster sugar

2 tbsp red pesto sauce

1 tbsp white or red wine vinegar

2 tbsp capers

6 tomatoes, skinned, halved and cut into thin wedges

1 can tuna fish in brine, about 200 g, drained and roughly flaked

6 black olives, stoned and halved

fresh flat-leaf parsley to garnish (optional)

Preparation time: 20–25 minutes, plus cooling

1 Cook the pasta in boiling water for 10–12 minutes, or according to the packet instructions, until al dente. Drain well, rinse with cold water and drain again very thoroughly.

2 While the pasta is cooking, heat half the oil in a saucepan. Add the onion and garlic, and fry for 3 minutes, stirring often. Add the remaining oil and the courgettes and cook, stirring occasionally, for 3 minutes.

3 Add the sugar, red pesto, vinegar and capers to the onion and courgettes. Heat for a few seconds, stirring until the ingredients have combined to form a dressing. Stir in the tomatoes, then transfer the mixture to a large mixing bowl and set aside to cool.

4 Add the drained pasta to the bowl, then gently mix in the tuna fish and black olives. Divide among 4 plates or transfer to a large serving bowl. Serve garnished with some flat-leaf parsley leaves, if liked.

Plus points

● Using tuna canned in water or brine, rather than in oil, keeps the fat content of the dish low.

● Tomatoes and courgettes together ensure that this simple salad provides an excellent supply of vitamin C.

Some more ideas

● To increase the fibre content and make a more substantial meal, add 1 can borlotti beans, about 400 g, drained, with the pasta. Omit the tuna for a vegetarian dish.

● Canned anchovies can be used instead of tuna. Drain the oil from 1 can, about 50 g, and use it instead of the olive oil for cooking the ingredients in step 1.

● Use 225 g (8 oz) small patty pan squash instead of courgettes. Trim their tops and bases, then slice them in half.

Each serving provides

kcal 420, **protein** 25 g, **fat** 12 g (of which saturated fat 2 g), **carbohydrate** 57 g (of which sugars 10 g), **fibre** 4 g

✓✓✓	C, selenium
✓✓	A
✓	B₁, E, folate, niacin, copper, potassium

for maximum vitality

52

Creamy turkey salad with grapes and pecans

With its wonderfully contrasting tastes and textures, this salad makes a satisfying main course that is luxurious without containing a lot of saturated fat. It is the perfect recipe for roast turkey leftovers or high-quality cooked turkey bought from the deli counter in the supermarket.

Serves 4

200 g (7 oz) fusilli (pasta spirals)

150 g (5½ oz) plain low-fat yogurt

3 tbsp mayonnaise

1 tsp white wine vinegar

2 tsp French mustard

3 tbsp chopped fresh tarragon

250 g (9 oz) skinless boneless roast turkey, cubed

2 celery sticks, cut into fine strips

115 g (4 oz) seedless black grapes, or a mixture of black and green grapes, halved

55 g (2 oz) pecan nuts, toasted and roughly chopped

salt and pepper

sprigs of fresh tarragon to garnish

To serve (optional)

mixed green salad

Preparation time: 25 minutes, plus cooling

Each serving provides

kcal 470, **protein** 28 g, **fat** 20 g (of which saturated fat 2.5 g), **carbohydrate** 46 g (of which sugars 9 g), **fibre** 2.5 g

✓✓✓	niacin
✓✓	B$_{12}$, E, copper
✓	B$_1$, B$_6$, calcium, iron, potassium, selenium

1 Cook the pasta in boiling water for 10–12 minutes, or according to the packet instructions, until al dente. Drain and rinse with cold water, then drain again and leave to cool.

2 Meanwhile, mix the yogurt with the mayonnaise, white wine vinegar, mustard and tarragon in a large bowl. Stir until all the ingredients are combined and the dressing is smooth.

3 Add the pasta, turkey, celery, grapes, toasted pecan nuts and seasoning to taste. Toss until the ingredients are all evenly coated with the creamy dressing.

4 Transfer to a serving dish or plates and garnish with sprigs of tarragon. Serve with a mixed green salad, if liked.

Plus points

- Turkey, without skin, is a first-class source of low-fat protein, and it contains more vitamin B$_{12}$, niacin and zinc than chicken.
- Black grapes provide useful amounts of bioflavonoids, the antioxidants that help to protect against the damaging effect of free radicals linked with cancer.

Some more ideas

- For a spicy Indian flavour, stir in 2 tbsp tikka masala curry paste (or to taste) with the yogurt. Garnish with chopped fresh coriander instead of the tarragon.
- Lower the fat content by using reduced-fat mayonnaise.
- Use 55 g (2 oz) natural roasted cashews instead of the pecans, and 2 cored and chopped dessert apples instead of the grapes. Add 55 g (2 oz) sultanas.
- Try 225 g (8 oz) firm smoked tofu instead of the turkey to make a tempting vegetarian salad.

for maximum vitality

Oriental chicken farfalle salad

Pasta bows taste deliciously different when combined with an exotic dressing of fish sauce, fresh red chilli and rice vinegar in a moist chicken salad. Fresh crunchy vegetables complete this well-balanced main-course dish. Any leftovers can be chilled – they will taste just as good the next day.

Serves 4

3 skinless boneless chicken breasts, about 150 g (5½ oz) each

2 lemon or lime slices

1 tbsp rice wine (sake or mirin) or dry sherry

300 g (10½ oz) farfalle (pasta bows)

150 g (5½ oz) carrots, cut into matchstick strips

1 red pepper, seeded and cut into matchstick strips

2 celery sticks, cut into matchstick strips

½ cucumber, about 200 g (7 oz), halved, seeded and cut into matchstick strips

Dressing

2 tbsp fish sauce

1 tsp caster sugar

1 tbsp rice vinegar, cider vinegar or white wine vinegar

1 tbsp soy sauce

1 small fresh red chilli, seeded and finely chopped

1 large garlic clove, crushed

Preparation time: 50 minutes, plus cooling, 1 hour marinating and about 30 minutes standing time

1 Place the chicken breasts in a large shallow pan and pour in enough water to cover them. Add the lemon or lime slices and the rice wine or sherry, and heat until just simmering. Reduce the heat and poach the chicken for 20 minutes or until cooked through. Remove from the heat and cover the pan, then leave the chicken to cool completely in the cooking liquid.

2 Meanwhile, cook the pasta in boiling water for 10–12 minutes, or according to the packet instructions, until al dente. Drain, rinse under cold running water and drain again. Set the pasta aside until cool.

3 Place the carrots, red pepper, celery and cucumber in a large salad bowl. To make the dressing, mix together the fish sauce and sugar, stirring until the sugar dissolves, then add the vinegar, soy sauce, chilli and garlic. Pour the dressing over the raw salad vegetables.

4 Drain the cooled chicken and pat dry on kitchen paper, then cut into bite-sized pieces. Stir the chicken and pasta into the dressed vegetables. Cover and leave to marinate in the fridge for about 1 hour. Bring the salad to room temperature before serving.

Some more ideas

• Use other pasta shapes such as amori or gemelli (narrow spirals).

• Make the salad with 600 g (1 lb 5 oz) white fish, such as haddock, plaice or whiting, instead of chicken. Poach the fish for 8–12 minutes or until just cooked and firm.

• Use peeled cooked prawns and/or crab meat (drained if canned) instead of chicken. Add a handful of bean sprouts to the other vegetables, if liked, and garnish the salad with chopped fresh herbs, such as mint, coriander or basil (Thai or ordinary basil).

Plus points

• Eaten without the skin, chicken is low in fat and the fat it does contain is mostly unsaturated.

• The combination of raw carrots, pepper and celery makes this salad an excellent source of vitamins, particularly vitamin C.

Each serving provides

kcal 435, **protein** 33 g, **fat** 7 g (of which saturated fat 2 g), **carbohydrate** 64 g (of which sugars 9 g), **fibre** 4.5 g

✓✓✓	A, C, niacin
✓✓	copper, selenium
✓	B₁, B₆, iron, potassium

for maximum vitality

56

Fruity pasta salad

Pineapple and pear give this salad a sweet accent, while a sprinkling of balsamic vinegar on the mixed salad leaves adds a delightful piquancy. With lean ham, a well-flavoured cheese, fruit and vegetables all adding their own nutrients to balance the pasta, the result is a marvellous dish for lunch or supper.

Serves 4

340 g (12 oz) mixed coloured pasta shapes

50 g (1¾ oz) fine green beans, topped and tailed

100 g (3½ oz) full-flavoured cheese, such as mature Cheddar or Leicester, diced

150 g (5½ oz) lean cooked ham, diced or cut into fine strips

100 g (3½ oz) peeled fresh pineapple, diced

½ small onion, finely chopped

3 tbsp mayonnaise

3 tbsp plain low-fat yogurt

½ tsp chopped piccalilli or pickled gherkin, or to taste (optional)

1 pear, peeled, cored and diced

1 tsp caster sugar, or to taste

juice of ¼ lemon, or to taste

cayenne pepper (optional)

125 g (4½ oz) mixed salad leaves, such as endive, lamb's lettuce, chicory, rocket, watercress or Japanese mizuna

1 tbsp sunflower oil (optional)

½ tsp balsamic vinegar, or to taste

2 tbsp coarsely chopped walnuts

2 tbsp dried cranberries (optional)

salt and pepper

Preparation time: 35 minutes

1 Cook the pasta in boiling water for 10–12 minutes, or according to the packet instructions, until al dente. Drain and rinse in cold water, then drain again.

2 Cook the beans in boiling water for about 3 minutes or until bright green and just tender, but still crisp. Drain and rinse under cold water, then drain again. Set aside.

3 Combine the cooked pasta with the cheese, ham, pineapple, onion, mayonnaise, yogurt, piccalilli or gherkin, pear and sugar. Add a little extra piccalilli or sugar, if liked. Mix well, then adjust the flavour of the dressing with lemon juice, seasoning and cayenne pepper, if using.

4 Dress the mixed salad leaves with the oil, if using, balsamic vinegar and a squeeze of lemon juice. Divide the dressed leaves among 4 plates and top with the pasta mixture.

5 Arrange the green beans, walnuts and dried cranberries, if using, around the leaves and serve immediately.

Plus points

- Cheese is a good source of protein and a valuable source of calcium, phosphorus, niacin and vitamin B_{12}.
- Using a strongly flavoured cheese, such as mature Cheddar, means that less is required for flavour in the dish, thus keeping the total fat content down.

Some more ideas

- Omit the piccalilli or gherkin and instead season the pasta with a sprinkling of curry powder, stirring it in well. Sprinkle with cashew nuts instead of walnuts.
- Reduced-fat mayonnaise can be used instead of the traditional type.
- Use 1 can chickpeas, about 400 g, well drained, instead of ham.
- Use 3 slices canned pineapple in natural juice, drained and diced, instead of fresh pineapple.

Each serving provides

kcal 655, **protein** 27 g, **fat** 29 g (of which saturated fat 9 g), **carbohydrate** 75 g (of which sugars 12 g), **fibre** 5 g

✓✓✓	calcium
✓✓	B_1, B_{12}, C, E, niacin, copper, selenium
✓	A, B_6, folate, iron, potassium

for maximum vitality

Lumache with cucumber salsa

Here little snail-shaped pasta, called lumache, trap a herby yogurt and tomato dressing so that each one is full of flavour. A refreshing vegetable and fruit salsa brings extra nutritional value as well as exciting taste and texture contrast. Offer warm crusty bread to mop up all the juices from the salsa.

for maximum vitality

Serves 4

225 g (8 oz) lumache (pasta snails) or other hollow shapes

4 tbsp chopped fresh parsley

4 tbsp chopped fresh mint

4 tbsp snipped fresh chives

2 tbsp chopped fresh tarragon

4 tomatoes, skinned, seeded and chopped

200 g (7 oz) plain low-fat yogurt

1 avocado

salt and pepper

sprigs of fresh mint to garnish

Cucumber salsa

4 celery sticks, finely diced

1 green pepper, seeded and finely diced or chopped

½ cucumber, diced or chopped

4 spring onions, finely sliced or chopped

grated zest of 1 lime (optional)

50 g (1¾ oz) watercress, coarsely chopped

100 g (3½ oz) ready-to-eat dried mango slices, diced

1 tbsp extra virgin olive oil

1 crisp sweet-sour dessert apple, such as Braeburn or Jonagold

Preparation time: 40–50 minutes, plus cooling and 1 hour optional chilling

1 Cook the pasta in boiling water for 10–12 minutes, or according to the packet instructions, until al dente.

2 Meanwhile, mix the parsley, mint, chives and tarragon with the tomatoes in a large bowl (the bowl should be large enough to take the cooked pasta too). Add a little seasoning and then stir in the yogurt.

3 Drain the cooked pasta thoroughly, shaking the shapes in a colander to make sure that there is no cooking water trapped in them. Add the hot pasta to the yogurt dressing and use a large spoon to turn them until they are thoroughly coated. Cover and set aside to cool until just warm. The pasta salad tastes good warm or it can be served cold, in which case leave to cool completely, then chill for 1 hour. The pasta can be dressed several hours in advance if this is more convenient.

4 Meanwhile, mix together the celery, green pepper, cucumber and spring onions. Stir in the lime zest, if using, the watercress and diced dried mango. Cover and set aside.

5 Shortly before serving, stir the oil into the cucumber mixture with seasoning to taste. Quarter, core and finely dice the apple, leaving its peel on. Add to the cucumber salsa and stir well so the apple is mixed in.

6 Halve the avocado and remove the stone, then cut it lengthways into quarters and peel off the skin. Dice the flesh and mix it into the pasta.

7 Serve the cucumber salsa as an accompaniment to the pasta so that it can be added to taste. (The hot pasta absorbs its yogurt dressing, becoming quite dry as it cools, so the cucumber salsa acts as a second dressing.) Garnish with sprigs of mint and serve immediately.

Plus points

• Vitamin C in fruit and vegetables is easily destroyed during cooking, so eating them raw ensures they provide the maximum of their vitamin content.

• The bacteria used to make yogurt are known to be helpful in maintaining the balance between 'friendly' and 'unfriendly' bacteria that live in the digestive tract.

Some more ideas

● This is an excellent recipe for wholemeal pasta or corn and vegetable pasta (useful for those on a gluten-free diet), as the firm texture and slightly nutty flavour balance the light, crunchy salsa.

● Add a finely chopped garlic clove to the yogurt dressing, if liked.

● Keep the yogurt dressing green by omitting the tomatoes, and make a red salsa using red pepper, instead of green, and a red-skinned apple. Add the tomatoes to the salsa and season it with a little paprika to warm both the flavour and colour.

● Other dried fruit can be used instead of mango. Dried pineapple and dried apricots are both delicious.

Each serving provides

kcal 410, **protein** 13 g, **fat** 12.5 g (of which saturated fat 3 g), **carbohydrate** 65 g (of which sugars 22.5 g), **fibre** 8 g

✓✓✓	C
✓✓	A, B₁, B₆, E, niacin, calcium, copper, iron, potassium
✓	folate, selenium

Rustic grilled vegetable and rigatoni salad

Grilled vegetables are delicious with chunky pasta in a tangy dressing. Serve this salad as a light lunch or offer it as an accompaniment for grilled poultry or meat, when it will serve 6 or 8.

Serves 4

200 g (7 oz) rigatoni
1 large red pepper, seeded and halved
125 g (4½ oz) tomatoes, cut into wedges
1 aubergine, trimmed and sliced lengthways
2 tbsp balsamic vinegar or lemon juice
3 tbsp extra virgin olive oil
2 tbsp shredded fresh basil
1 tbsp chopped capers
1 large garlic clove, crushed (optional)
30 g (1 oz) Parmesan cheese, freshly grated
salt and pepper

Preparation time: 35 minutes, plus cooling and 30 minutes marinating

Each serving provides Ⓥ

kcal 310, **protein** 10 g, **fat** 12 g (of which saturated fat 3 g), **carbohydrate** 42 g (of which sugars 5.5 g), **fibre** 3 g

✓✓	A, C
✓	niacin, calcium, copper, potassium

1 Cook the rigatoni in boiling water for 10–12 minutes, or according to the packet instructions, until al dente. Drain and rinse under cold running water, then drain thoroughly and set aside to cool.

2 Preheat the grill to high. Grill the pepper halves, skin side up, for 5–10 minutes or until blistered and blackened. Place in a polythene bag, then leave until cool enough to handle.

3 Grill the tomatoes and aubergine for about 5 minutes or until slightly charred. Turn the vegetables so that they cook evenly, and remove the pieces as they are ready. Place the tomato wedges in a large salad bowl. Set the aubergine slices aside on a plate to cool slightly.

4 Cut the aubergine slices into 2.5 cm (1 in) strips and add to the tomatoes. Peel the peppers and cut them into 2.5 cm (1 in) strips, then add to the salad bowl. Mix in the pasta.

5 In a small bowl, mix the balsamic vinegar or lemon juice with the olive oil, basil, capers, garlic, if using, and Parmesan cheese. Lightly toss this dressing into the salad. Season to taste. Set the salad aside to marinate for about 30 minutes so that the flavours can mingle before serving.

Plus points

- Aubergines are a useful vegetable for making satisfying meals without a high calorie content. They contain just 15 kcal per 100 g (3½ oz).
- Grilling or baking is a healthy cooking method for vegetables like aubergines, which can absorb large amounts of fat when they are fried.
- Adding a little Parmesan cheese to pasta dishes contributes useful calcium as well as a wonderful flavour.

Some more ideas

- For a hearty vegetarian main course salad, stir in 1 can cannellini or red kidney beans, about 400 g, well drained.
- Grilled courgettes and asparagus can be added to the salad. Slice the courgettes lengthways. Grill alongside the aubergine and tomatoes.
- Replace the aubergine with well-drained, bottled char-grilled artichokes.

Penne rigati with sesame and orange dressing

This fresh-flavoured pasta salad is ideal as a side dish with grilled chicken or firm fish, such as fresh tuna or swordfish. It makes a healthy change from noodles dressed with oil or butter and Parmesan cheese.

Serves 4

200 g (7 oz) penne rigati (ridged penne)

2 large oranges

6 spring onions, cut into short fine strips

55 g (2 oz) bean sprouts

2 tbsp sesame seeds, toasted

Dressing

grated zest and juice of 1 orange

1 tbsp toasted sesame oil

2 tbsp light soy sauce

1 garlic clove, crushed

1 tbsp finely grated fresh root ginger

salt and pepper

Preparation time: 25–30 minutes, plus cooling

Each serving provides Ⓥ

kcal 280, **protein** 9 g, **fat** 8 g (of which saturated fat 1 g), **carbohydrate** 45 g (of which sugars 8 g), **fibre** 4 g

✓✓✓	C
✓✓	copper
✓	B$_1$, folate, niacin, potassium, selenium

---

1 Cook the pasta in boiling water for 10–12 minutes, or according to the packet instructions, until al dente.

2 While the pasta is cooking, peel the oranges, removing all the pith. Holding the oranges over a bowl to catch any juice, cut out the segments from their surrounding membrane. Set the segments aside, and reserve the juice in the bowl.

3 Place the spring onion strips in a bowl of cold water and set them aside until they curl.

4 To make the dressing, add the orange zest and juice to the juices reserved from segmenting the oranges. Add the sesame oil, soy sauce, garlic, grated fresh ginger and seasoning to taste. Whisk lightly to mix.

5 Drain the pasta and add to the dressing. Mix well, then cover and set aside to cool.

6 When ready to serve, thoroughly drain the spring onions; reserve a few for garnish and add the remainder to the salad together with the orange segments, bean sprouts and toasted sesame seeds. Gently toss the ingredients together, then serve the salad immediately, sprinkled with the reserved spring onions.

Some more ideas

• Use Japanese soba noodles, made from buckwheat flour, instead of penne and cook them for 5–7 minutes. Use sunflower oil in the dressing instead of the sesame oil and omit the sesame seeds. Stir in 1 tbsp Thai red curry paste instead of the fresh root ginger. Add 2 tbsp finely chopped fresh coriander with the orange segments, if liked.

• To increase the vegetable content of the salad, finely shred ½ bulb fennel and add it to the salad; scatter with the fronds or feathery leaves from the fennel to garnish.

Plus points

• Oranges are an excellent source of vitamin C, with 1 orange providing more than twice the recommended daily intake of the vitamin. A recently published study showed a connection between a regular intake of vitamin C and the maintenance of intellectual function in elderly people. Those eating a diet rich in vitamin C were also less likely to suffer a stroke.

• Oranges, and other citrus fruit, also contain coumarins, compounds that are believed to help thin the blood and thus prevent stroke and heart attacks.

Radiatori with flageolet beans in tomato dressing

When beans and pasta are eaten together, the vegetable proteins combine to provide as good a source of protein as meat. Here, tender flageolet beans partner chunky pasta shapes in a salad with celery, red pepper and canned artichoke hearts. A well-flavoured dressing marries the ingredients perfectly.

Serves 4

225 g (8 oz) radiatori (pasta grills) or other shapes

1 can artichoke hearts, about 400 g, drained and quartered

4 ripe tomatoes, skinned and cut into thin wedges

3 celery sticks, thinly sliced

1 red pepper, seeded and cut into thin strips

1 can flageolet beans, about 400 g, drained and rinsed

2 tbsp finely shredded fresh basil

Tomato dressing

2 tbsp sun-dried tomato paste

1 garlic clove, crushed

2 tbsp extra virgin olive oil

2 tbsp lemon juice

1 tsp caster sugar

salt and pepper

Preparation time: 25–35 minutes, plus cooling

Each serving provides (V)

kcal 400, **protein** 18.5 g, **fat** 7.5 g (of which saturated fat 1.5 g), **carbohydrate** 68 g (of which sugars 10 g), **fibre** 9 g

✓✓✓	A, C
✓✓	B₁, B₆, niacin, iron, potassium
✓	E, copper, selenium

1 Cook the pasta in boiling water for 10–12 minutes, or according to the packet instructions, until al dente. Drain the pasta thoroughly and turn it into a large bowl.

2 Add the artichoke hearts, tomatoes, celery, red pepper, flageolet beans and basil. Gently toss the pasta and vegetables together. The cold vegetables will cool the pasta, keeping the pieces firm and separate, while the warmth of the pasta will bring out the flavours of the vegetables.

3 Whisk all the ingredients for the dressing together until thoroughly blended. Add seasoning to taste and pour the dressing over the salad. Lightly toss the salad to coat all the ingredients with dressing, then set aside until cool. Transfer the salad to individual bowls or one large dish to serve.

Some more ideas

• Try canned soya beans instead of flageolet. These small, firm and nutty beans are an excellent source of vegetable protein.

• Omit the tomatoes, and instead add a quartered and thinly sliced bulb of fennel. Replace the flageolet with cannellini beans. Add 55 g (2 oz) finely shredded Italian salami to make a meaty main course salad.

• Marinate 225 g (8 oz) button mushrooms with the basil in the dressing for at least 2 hours before making the salad, then add them instead of the canned artichoke hearts. Add halved cherry tomatoes instead of the large tomatoes, and omit the celery.

Plus points

• Flageolet beans are high in protein and low in fat, and they also provide useful amounts of vitamin B₁ and iron. Along with other beans and pulses, they are a good source of dietary fibre, particularly soluble fibre, which can help to reduce cholesterol levels in the blood and thus lessen the risk of heart disease.

Saffron couscous with peppers

Serve this salad warm or cool as a main dish for 4, or as a main course accompaniment for 6. Either way, it is a flavoursome low-fat vegetarian dish that has real meal appeal. Saffron, which brings the taste and colour of the Middle East to the couscous, is readily available from larger supermarkets.

Serves 4

1 large garlic clove, crushed
3 tbsp extra virgin olive oil
4 large sprigs of fresh rosemary
1 large yellow pepper, seeded and cut into wide strips
1 large red pepper, seeded and cut into wide strips
2 courgettes, halved lengthways, then cut into 2.5 cm (1 in) chunks
4½ tsp lemon juice
harissa or other chilli sauce, to taste
2 tomatoes, skinned, seeded and diced
large handful of fresh coriander leaves, mint or parsley, or a combination of these, coarsely chopped
salt and pepper

Couscous

550 ml (19 fl oz) vegetable stock
10–12 saffron threads
340 g (12 oz) couscous
1 bay leaf, torn in half
50 g (1¾ oz) raisins or sultanas
15 g (½ oz) butter
2 spring onions, trimmed and finely chopped

Preparation time: about 1 hour, plus optional cooling

1 Preheat the oven to 200°C (400°F, gas mark 6). Place the garlic and oil in a small bowl and set aside to infuse while the oven heats. Lay the rosemary sprigs in a roasting tin.

2 Meanwhile, for the couscous, put the stock and saffron in a saucepan. Bring to the boil, then cover, remove from the heat and leave to infuse.

3 Using your hands, rub the pepper and courgette pieces with a little of the garlic-flavoured oil so they are well coated. Place the peppers in the roasting tin on top of the rosemary and roast for 10 minutes. Then add the courgettes and continue roasting for 20–25 minutes, turning the vegetables over once or twice, until they are just tender and slightly charred.

4 Pour the remaining garlic-infused oil into a large bowl. Whisk in the lemon juice, and harissa and seasoning to taste to make a dressing.

5 As soon as the vegetables are cooked, transfer them to the bowl containing the dressing and add the tomatoes. Stir to coat with the dressing, then set aside to cool.

6 Bring the saffron-infused stock to the boil. Add the couscous, bay leaf and raisins or sultanas. Stir well, then cover and remove from the heat. Leave to stand for 5 minutes.

7 Add the butter to the couscous and place over a moderate heat. Cook for 1–2 minutes, fluffing with a fork to separate the grains. Remove the bay leaf. Stir in the spring onions and season to taste. Leave the cousous to cool until just warm or allow it to cool completely, as preferred.

8 Place the couscous on a serving platter. Top with the vegetables and any dressing remaining in the bowl, scatter the chopped herbs over and serve. Lightly grilled pitta bread, cut into strips, is the ideal accompaniment.

Plus points

● Couscous is low in fat and high in carbohydrate and fibre. Mixing couscous with delicious roasted vegetables makes a main dish that can be a lower fat alternative to a lamb stew and couscous.

● Weight for weight, peppers contain over twice as much vitamin C as oranges. Although some of the vitamin C will be destroyed during cooking, useful amounts will remain.

Some more ideas

• For a heartier dish, add 1 can chickpeas, butter beans or flageolet beans, about 400 g, drained and rinsed, to the hot vegetables.

• For a meat-based main course, add spicy roasted lamb. Combine 2 tsp extra virgin olive oil with 1 tsp each ground coriander and cumin and a pinch of cayenne pepper. Rub this mixture over 400 g (14 oz) well-trimmed lamb neck fillets and marinate for 30 minutes. When the vegetables are cooked, place the lamb on a rack in a roasting tin and roast for about 12 minutes. Remove from the oven and leave to rest for 5 minutes, then slice thinly.

Each serving provides

kcal 375, **protein** 8 g, **fat** 13 g (of which saturated fat 3.5 g), **carbohydrate** 60 g (of which sugars 16 g), **fibre** 2.5 g

✓✓✓	A, C
✓	B₁, B₆, copper, potassium

Fast Pasta

Nourishing dishes made in under 30 minutes

WHEN YOU'RE HUNGRY BUT IN A HURRY, pasta is a perfect choice. It takes almost no time at all to toss linguine with pan-fried salmon chunks, or penne with fresh young spring vegetables. Pasta is the ideal partner for speedy stir-fries – flat rice sticks with spicy tiger prawns, fine rice vermicelli with steak and mushrooms, egg noodles with strips of pork and green vegetables. Another quick and tasty idea from the Orient is Japanese soba noodles in a savoury broth with tofu and vegetables. And combining pasta and cheese makes super-fast nutritious meals – pasta tubes with feta, chickpeas and rocket, or tagliatelle with creamy goat's cheese and toasted nuts.

Linguine with pan-fried salmon

All the ingredients for this dish are quickly assembled and cooked, and the result is truly delicious as well as visually impressive. This is definitely a dish to convince anyone who has doubts about the taste benefits of well-balanced eating. With bread and salad, it makes a hearty meal.

Serves 4

400 g (14 oz) salmon fillet, skinned

grated zest and juice of 1 lemon

2 tbsp chopped fresh dill

340 g (12 oz) linguine

225 g (8 oz) carrots, cut into matchstick strips

225 g (8 oz) courgettes, cut into matchstick strips

1 tsp sunflower oil

100 g (3½ oz) reduced-fat crème fraîche

salt and pepper

To garnish

sprigs of fresh dill (optional)

1 lemon, cut into wedges

Preparation time: 10 minutes, plus optional marinating

Cooking time: 15 minutes

Each serving provides

kcal 560, **protein** 33 g, **fat** 18 g (of which saturated fat 5 g), **carbohydrate** 70 g (of which sugars 6 g), **fibre** 4.5 g

✓✓✓	A, B₁₂, niacin
✓✓	B₁, B₆, C, copper, selenium
✓	E, folate, potassium

1 Cut the salmon into chunks and place in a dish. Add the lemon zest and juice, and the dill. Turn the chunks of salmon to coat them evenly. If time permits, cover and marinate in the fridge for at least 10 minutes.

2 Cook the linguine in boiling water for 10 minutes, or according to the packet instructions, until al dente. Add the carrots to the pasta after 8 minutes cooking, then add the courgettes 1 minute later.

3 Meanwhile, brush a non-stick or heavy-based frying pan with the oil and heat thoroughly. Drain the salmon, reserving the lemon juice marinade. Add the salmon to the hot pan and cook, turning the pieces occasionally, for 3–4 minutes, or until the fish is firm and just cooked.

4 Add the reserved marinade and the crème fraîche to the salmon, and cook for a few seconds. Remove from the heat and stir in seasoning to taste.

5 Drain the pasta and vegetables, and transfer them to a serving dish or to individual plates. Add the salmon mixture, garnish with fresh dill, if liked, and serve with lemon wedges.

Plus points

● Salmon is an oily fish rich in omega-3 fatty acids, which can help to reduce the risk of heart disease.

● Cutting the courgettes and carrots into thin, pasta-like strips and mixing them with pasta is a good way of presenting them to children who are reluctant to eat vegetables.

Some more ideas

● Trout fillets, asparagus tips and broad beans are an excellent alternative combination to the salmon, carrot and courgette. Cook the asparagus tips and beans with the pasta for the last 4–5 minutes.

● Use the recipe as a basis for a quick, healthy storecupboard supper dish, adding frozen green beans and sweetcorn to the pasta, and using well-drained canned salmon instead of the fresh fish. There is no need to marinate or cook the canned salmon: the heat of the pasta will bring out its flavour beautifully.

Chilli prawns with rice sticks

Rice sticks are flat noodles made from rice flour, available from Oriental food stores. With a lighter texture than wheat-flour noodles, they are perfect for stir-fries. Here, fine asparagus, succulent tiger prawns and crunchy water chestnuts are cooked quickly with the tender noodles.

Serves 4

200 g (7 oz) rice sticks

2 tbsp sunflower oil

200 g (7 oz) raw tiger prawns, peeled

3 garlic cloves, cut into fine shreds

1 fresh red chilli, halved, seeded and thinly sliced

1 tbsp finely chopped fresh root ginger

100 g (3½ oz) extra fine asparagus, cut into 5 cm (2 in) lengths

150 g (5½ oz) trimmed sugarsnap peas, cut into shreds

1 can water chestnuts, about 225 g, drained and halved

4 spring onions, cut into strips

2 tsp ground coriander

4 tbsp fish sauce

1 tbsp clear honey

1½ tsp cornflour

15 g (½ oz) fresh coriander, finely chopped
fresh coriander to garnish (optional)

Preparation time: 15 minutes
Cooking time: 10 minutes

Each serving provides

kcal 345, protein 14.5 g, fat 6 g (of which saturated fat 0.5 g), carbohydrate 58 g (of which sugars 7 g), fibre 1.5 g

✓✓✓	B$_{12}$, C
✓✓	copper
✓	iron, selenium

1 Cook or soak the noodles according to the packet instructions. Drain well and set aside.

2 Heat 1 tbsp oil in a wok or large frying pan, then stir-fry the prawns for just a few minutes, until they turn from blue-grey to pink. Use a draining spoon to transfer the prawns to a plate.

3 Add the remaining oil to the wok and heat briefly, then add the garlic, chilli and ginger. Stir for a few seconds to flavour the oil, but take care not to let the flavourings burn.

4 Toss the asparagus, sugarsnap peas and water chestnuts into the wok. Stir-fry for about 3 minutes or until the asparagus and sugarsnaps start to soften. Add the spring onions and ground coriander and stir to mix.

5 Mix the fish sauce, honey and cornflour with 2 tbsp water, then pour into the wok and stir gently until boiling and thickened.

6 Return the prawns to the wok and add the noodles and chopped coriander. Toss gently until the ingredients are evenly combined and everything is hot. Serve immediately, garnished with coriander leaves, if liked.

Plus points

● Prawns are low in fat, but high in protein. They contain useful amounts of many of the B vitamins, particularly vitamin B$_{12}$, essential for the formation of red blood cells and for maintaining a healthy nervous system. Prawns are also a good source of the antioxidant selenium.

Another idea

● Use 2 skinless boneless chicken breasts (fillets) instead of the prawns; cut them into thin strips. Instead of the asparagus, sugarsnap peas and water chestnuts, use 1 seeded and diced red pepper, 125 g (4½ oz) sliced baby corn and 1 can bamboo shoots, about 225 g, drained and cut into shreds. Substitute Chinese five-spice powder and fresh basil for the ground and fresh coriander.

fast pasta

Hot pasta with pickled herrings in a dill and mustard dressing

Marinated herrings are an excellent standby ingredient as an alternative to canned fish – there are many bottled varieties that keep well in the fridge for 2–3 months. They are delicious in this Scandinavian-inspired dish, which combines them with hot pasta and crunchy red onion. Serve rye bread as an accompaniment.

Serves 4

1 jar marinated herring fillets in vinegar with crisp onion and spices, about 275 g, drained

75 g (2½ oz) large pickled gherkins, drained and cut into thin strips

1 small red onion, thinly sliced

4 tomatoes, seeded and diced

1 tbsp mild Swedish or French mustard

4 tbsp clear apple juice

2 tbsp extra virgin olive oil

1 tbsp chopped fresh dill or 1 tsp dried dill

340 g (12 oz) dischi volanti (small pasta discs) or other shapes

salt and pepper

sprigs of fresh dill to garnish (optional)

Preparation time: 10 minutes

Cooking time: 10–12 minutes

Each serving provides

kcal 520, **protein** 23 g, **fat** 15 g (of which saturated fat 1 g), **carbohydrate** 78 g (of which sugars 14 g), **fibre** 4 g

✓✓✓	C
✓✓	niacin, copper, selenium
✓	B₁, iron, potassium

1 Cut the herrings diagonally into thin strips, place in a bowl and add the gherkins. Mix in half the red onion and the diced tomatoes.

2 Whisk the mustard, apple juice, oil, dill and seasoning together. Pour this dressing over the herring mixture and stir to mix well. Cover and set aside while cooking the pasta, so that the flavours can mingle and develop.

3 Cook the pasta in boiling water for 10–12 minutes, or according to the packet instructions, until al dente. Towards the end of the cooking time for the pasta, drain the dressing off the herring mixture.

4 Drain the pasta well and turn into a serving bowl. Add the dressing from the herring mixture and toss well to coat evenly. Arrange the herring mixture on top. Garnish with the remaining onion and sprigs of dill, if using, then serve immediately.

Plus points

● Herring and mackerel are rich in omega-3 fatty acids, a type of polyunsaturated fat thought to help to protect against coronary heart disease and strokes by making the blood less 'sticky' and therefore less likely to clot. A diet rich in omega-3 fatty acids may also be helpful in preventing and treating arthritis. Current healthy eating guidelines recommend eating oily fish such as herring and mackerel at least twice a week.

Some more ideas

● Smoked mackerel can be used instead of herrings, and olives instead of gherkins.

● Wholemeal pasta goes well with full-flavoured smoked mackerel and is a good way to increase the fibre content of the dish.

Stir-fried beef with fine noodles

Tangy tamarind and lemongrass infuse a Thai-inspired sauce for tender strips of beef and fine rice noodles.
Chilli brings a little heat. With mange-tout and baby sweetcorn adding pleasing colour and crunch, as well
as all-important vegetable balance, this is a quick and easy dish that is a meal in itself.

Serves 2

1 tsp tamarind paste

3 tbsp boiling water

2 tbsp soy sauce

2 tsp toasted sesame oil

1 tbsp rice wine (sake or mirin) or sherry

100 g (3½ oz) fine rice noodles, such as
    vermicelli

1 tbsp sunflower oil

225 g (8 oz) lean rump steak, cut into strips

85 g (3 oz) onion, cut into wedges

2 tsp chopped lemongrass

1 fresh red chilli, seeded and chopped

2 large garlic cloves, crushed

85 g (3 oz) mange-tout, halved diagonally

6 baby sweetcorn, sliced

100 g (3½ oz) fresh shiitake or chestnut
    mushrooms, sliced

To serve

soy sauce

Preparation time: 20 minutes

Cooking time: 10 minutes

Each serving provides

kcal 460, **protein** 30 g, **fat** 15 g (of which
saturated fat 3 g), **carbohydrate** 49 g (of
which sugars 6.5 g), **fibre** 3 g

✓✓✓	B₁₂, C, niacin, copper
✓✓	iron, zinc, potassium
✓	B₁, B₂, B₆

1 In a small bowl, combine the tamarind paste and boiling water and leave to soak for 10 minutes, stirring frequently to break down the paste. Mix the resulting tamarind liquid with the soy sauce, sesame oil and rice wine or sherry.

2 While the tamarind is soaking, soak the rice noodles in boiling water for 4 minutes, or according to the packet instructions. Then drain, rinse under cold running water and set aside to drain thoroughly.

3 Heat the sunflower oil in a wok or very large frying pan and stir-fry the beef over a high heat for about 3 minutes or until cooked. Use a draining spoon to remove the beef from the wok and set it aside.

4 Add the onion, lemongrass, chilli and garlic to the wok and stir-fry over a high heat for 1 minute. Add the mange-tout, sweetcorn and mushrooms, and continue stir-frying for 2 minutes.

5 Return the beef to the wok. Add the tamarind liquid and the noodles and stir for about 1 minute to heat through. Serve immediately, offering soy sauce for extra seasoning as required.

Plus points

• Mushrooms provide useful amounts of the B vitamins niacin and B₂. They are also a good source of copper, which is important for healthy bones and to help the body to absorb iron from food.

• Onions contain allicin, which has anti-fungal and antibiotic properties.

Some more ideas

• Use strips of chicken breast instead of beef.

• Other vegetables that work well in the stir-fry include strips of red or green pepper, sliced canned water chestnuts, chopped or shredded spring onions and bean sprouts.

fast pasta

Hong Kong-style chow mein with pork and green vegetables

A mixture of green vegetables adds colour, crispness and food value to this simple noodle stir-fry with pork and dried mushrooms. Chinese egg noodles are prepared more quickly than Western pasta – they only need brief soaking – so this dish can be made from start to finish in less than 30 minutes.

Serves 4

25 g (scant 1 oz) dried Chinese mushrooms or shiitake

chicken or vegetable stock (optional – see method)

340 g (12 oz) Chinese egg noodles

2 tbsp sunflower oil

1 large garlic clove, crushed

1 tbsp finely chopped fresh root ginger

1 fresh red or green chilli, seeded and finely chopped, or to taste

2 tsp five-spice powder

200 g (7 oz) pork fillet, trimmed and cut into strips

2 green peppers, seeded and thinly sliced

100 g (3½ oz) small broccoli florets

2 celery sticks, thinly sliced

2 tbsp soy sauce

1 tbsp rice wine (sake or mirin) or dry sherry

100 g (3½ oz) bean sprouts

2 tbsp finely chopped fresh coriander

2 tsp toasted sesame oil

fresh coriander leaves to garnish

Preparation time: about 20 minutes
Cooking time: about 6 minutes

1 Place the mushrooms in a small bowl and pour in enough boiling water to cover them. Leave to soak for 10 minutes. Line a sieve with muslin or kitchen paper and place it over a bowl, then pour the mushrooms and their soaking liquid into it. Measure the strained liquid and make it up to 100 ml (3½ fl oz) with chicken or vegetable stock if necessary, then set aside. Discard any tough stalks from the mushrooms, slice them and set aside.

2 While the mushrooms are soaking, place the noodles in a large mixing bowl and pour in enough boiling water to cover them generously. Leave to soak for 4 minutes, or according to the packet instructions, until tender. Drain well and set aside.

3 Heat a wok or large frying pan over a high heat. Add 1 tbsp of the sunflower oil and, when it is hot, stir in the garlic, ginger, chilli and five-spice powder. Stir-fry for 30 seconds, taking care not to let the flavourings burn.

4 Add the strips of pork and continue stir-frying for about 2 minutes or until they are cooked through. Use a draining spoon to remove the pork from the wok and set it aside.

5 Add the remaining oil to the wok and heat until it is almost smoking. Stir in the peppers, broccoli, celery and mushrooms, and stir-fry for 2 minutes. Stir in the mushroom liquid, soy sauce and rice wine or sherry, then return the pork to the wok. Continue cooking, stirring constantly, for about 1 minute or until the pork is reheated.

6 Stir in the noodles, then the bean sprouts and toss together briefly, just long enough to heat the ingredients without softening the bean sprouts, as they should retain their crunch.

7 Stir in the chopped coriander and sprinkle with the sesame oil. Serve the chow mein immediately, garnished with coriander leaves.

Plus points

• The average fat content of lean pork is just 3.5% (3.5 g per 100 g), much the same as that contained in chicken breast, which (without skin) contains 3.2 g per 100 g. Pork is also a good source of zinc, and it provides useful amounts of iron and the B vitamins, particularly B_1, B_6, B_{12} and niacin.

Some more ideas

● Replace the pork with skinless boneless chicken breasts (fillets), cut into thin slices, or peeled raw tiger prawns.

● Use wheat-free Chinese rice noodles for anyone on a gluten-free diet.

● For a delicious vegetarian version, omit the pork fillet and add 300 g (10½ oz) mange-tout or sugarsnap peas. Baby sweetcorn, halved lengthways, sliced carrots, chopped French beans, cauliflower florets and sliced fresh mushrooms are also all suitable.

Each serving provides

kcal 488, **protein** 17 g, **fat** 13 g (of which saturated fat 3 g), **carbohydrate** 73 g (of which sugars 3 g), **fibre** 2.5 g

✓✓✓	C
✓✓	B₁, B₁₂, niacin
✓	B₆, folate, iron, potassium, zinc

fast pasta

Pasta with fresh sage, rocket and feta cheese

This quick main dish can be served hot or cool. The pasta is topped with feta cheese, which has a fresh, salty flavour that goes well with pancetta, the Italian bacon, chickpeas and tomato in the sauce. For best results, use a tubular or thick pasta shape that will complement the chunky sauce.

Serves 4

400 g (14 oz) tubular pasta shapes, such as casarecce (slim rolls), penne or macaroni

50 g (1¾ oz) pancetta, finely chopped

2 garlic cloves, finely chopped (optional)

2 shallots, finely chopped

8 fresh sage leaves, shredded

1 can chickpeas, about 400 g, drained

1 can chopped tomatoes, about 400 g

pinch of sugar

50 g (1¾ oz) rocket, stalks removed if preferred

100 g (3½ oz) feta cheese, crumbled

pepper

Preparation time: 10 minutes

Cooking time: about 20 minutes

1 Cook the pasta in boiling water for 10–12 minutes, or according to the packet instructions, until al dente. Drain well.

2 While the pasta is cooking, heat a large frying pan over a moderately high heat. Add the pancetta, garlic, if using, shallots and sage, and cook, stirring frequently, for 6–8 minutes or until the pancetta is golden brown and the shallots are soft.

3 Add the chickpeas, tomatoes with their juice and the sugar, and bring to the boil. Reduce the heat and simmer for 10 minutes or until the sauce has thickened slightly. Season with pepper (there is no need for salt as feta cheese is quite salty).

4 Stir in the pasta until it is well coated with the sauce ingredients. Add the rocket and stir in lightly, then sprinkle with the feta cheese and serve.

Some more ideas

● Use finely shredded radicchio or baby spinach instead of rocket. Adding the greens at the last minute preserves both their texture and vitamin content.

● To increase the fibre content, use wholemeal shapes or noodles. Wholemeal pasta will taste good with the rich sauce and sharp cheese.

● For a vegetarian dish, omit the pancetta and use 2 cans of chickpeas.

● Fresh sage has a natural affinity with beans, so try cannellini, flageolet, borlotti or butter beans instead of the chickpeas. Canned beans are quick and convenient, but dried beans, soaked and cooked, will have a better texture.

Each serving provides

kcal 600, **protein** 26 g, **fat** 15 g (of which saturated fat 6 g), **carbohydrate** 96 g (of which sugars 6.5 g), **fibre** 8 g

✓✓	C, E, niacin, calcium, iron, copper, selenium
✓	B₁, folate, potassium

Plus points

● Feta cheese is high in fat and salt, but because it has such a strong flavour, a little goes a long way. Like all cheese it is a good source of protein, calcium and phosphorus, and it provides useful amounts of B vitamins and vitamin E.

fast pasta

82

Teriyaki-style noodles with tofu

This rich Japanese-style broth, flavoured with vibrant fresh herbs, ginger and garlic, peps up firm, white cubes of tofu and long strands of earthy buckwheat noodles. It is a delicious low-fat vegetarian recipe for protein-rich tofu. Serve it for lunch or supper, with fresh fruit to follow.

Serves 2

150 g (5½ oz) soba (Japanese buckwheat noodles)

225 g (8 oz) mixed vegetables, such as asparagus tips, broccoli, carrots, cauliflower, green beans or mange-tout

100 ml (3½ fl oz) light soy sauce

300 ml (10 fl oz) vegetable stock

4 tbsp rice wine (sake or mirin) or dry sherry

280 g (10 oz) firm tofu, diced

2 spring onions, chopped

1 fresh red chilli, seeded and chopped

1 heaped tbsp chopped fresh mint

1 heaped tbsp chopped fresh coriander

1 large garlic clove, crushed

½ tsp grated fresh root ginger

2 tsp toasted sesame oil (optional)

Preparation time: 15 minutes
Cooking time: 10 minutes

1 Bring a large saucepan of water to the boil and cook the soba noodles for about 6 minutes, or according to the packet instructions, until al dente.

2 Meanwhile, cut all the mixed vegetables into bite-sized pieces. Add them to the simmering pasta for the final 3–4 minutes of cooking.

3 Drain the pasta and vegetables in a large colander. Place all the remaining ingredients in the empty saucepan and return it to the heat. Heat until simmering, then reduce the heat to the minimum setting. Return the pasta and vegetables to the pan, and cook very briefly until they are reheated.

4 Serve in deep soup bowls, with a spoon to drink the tasty broth and a fork or chopsticks for picking up the solid ingredients.

Plus points

- Evidence is accumulating from around the world to suggest that eating soya beans and soya products, such as tofu, may help to reduce the risk of certain cancers, heart disease and osteoporosis, as well as helping to alleviate symptoms associated with the menopause.

Some more ideas

- Replace the tofu with 225 g (8 oz) peeled cooked prawns or diced, skinned, cooked chicken or turkey.
- Fresh basil can be used in place of, or in addition to, the mint and coriander, and pumpkin seed oil or walnut oil can be added instead of sesame oil.
- Wheat-flour or rice noodles such as rice sticks can be used in place of soba noodles, but adjust the cooking time according to the instructions on the packet.

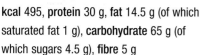

Each serving provides

kcal 495, **protein** 30 g, **fat** 14.5 g (of which saturated fat 1 g), **carbohydrate** 65 g (of which sugars 4.5 g), **fibre** 5 g

✓✓✓ C, calcium, iron

✓✓ B₁, E, niacin, folate, copper, potassium

fast pasta

Pasta with potato, beans and pesto

This is a traditional Ligurian dish that is usually made with potatoes, green beans and baby broad beans. Here, broccoli and courgettes boost the green vegetable content. The pesto sauce used to dress the pasta and vegetables is lighter than most, but still packs a wonderful flavoursome punch.

Serves 4

600 g (1 lb 5 oz) small new potatoes, halved or quartered

225 g (8 oz) broccoli, cut into small florets

75 g (2½ oz) shelled broad beans, skinned if preferred, 340–400 g (12–14 oz) in pods

170 g (6 oz) fine green beans, topped and tailed

2 courgettes, cut into bite-sized chunks

300 g (10½ oz) tubular or hollow pasta shapes, such as casarecce (slim rolled lengths), gemelli (narrow spirals), orecchiette (little ears) or gnocchi (fluted shells)

sprigs of fresh basil to garnish

Tomato pesto sauce

4–5 garlic cloves, coarsely chopped

2 tbsp pine nuts

100 g (3½ oz) fresh basil leaves

55 g (2 oz) Parmesan cheese, freshly grated

4 tbsp extra virgin olive oil

2 ripe tomatoes, diced

salt

Preparation time: 10 minutes

Cooking time: about 20 minutes

1 Cook the potatoes in boiling water for about 15 minutes or until they are tender, but not soft. Add the broccoli, broad beans, green beans and courgettes, and simmer all together for a further 5 minutes.

2 Meanwhile, cook the pasta in boiling water for 10–12 minutes, or according to the packet instructions, until al dente.

3 Make the pesto sauce while the vegetables and pasta are cooking. Pound the garlic with a pinch of salt and the pine nuts in a mortar using a pestle. Add the basil and continue pounding until the ingredients form a green paste, then work in the Parmesan cheese and oil. Finally, work in the tomatoes. Alternatively, the pesto can be made in a food processor or blender: put all the ingredients, except the oil, in the container and whiz to a paste, then gradually add the oil through the feed tube with the motor running.

4 Drain the pasta and vegetables and toss both together. Top with the pesto, garnish with sprigs of basil, scattering them over the top, and serve immediately.

Some more ideas

● For a more concentrated basil flavour, omit the tomato and Parmesan from the pesto sauce. Toss the pesto with the pasta and vegetables, and serve topped with dollops of soft mild goat's cheese.

● For a Sicilian-style pesto, use blanched almonds instead of the pine nuts. Cut them into fine slivers and add to the pounded mixture.

● To boost the flavour, especially when fresh basil is not at its best, add a few sprigs of fresh mint, flat-leaf parsley and/or rocket to the pesto.

Plus points

● Garlic contains a phytochemical called allicin, which has anti-fungal and antibiotic properties. It can also help to reduce high blood cholesterol levels and inhibit blood clotting, thereby reducing the risk of heart attack and stroke.

Each serving provides

kcal 660, **protein** 25 g, **fat** 24 g (of which saturated fat 5.5 g), **carbohydrate** 90 g (of which sugars 7 g), **fibre** 9 g

✓✓✓	C, calcium
✓✓	A, B₁, B₆, E, folate, niacin, copper, iron, potassium
✓	selenium

fast pasta

87

Penne primavera

This classic Italian dish is intended to make the very most of young spring produce, freshly picked from the vegetable plot. With today's choice of vegetables in supermarkets, the selection can be varied for year-round meals, and the recipe can also be made as a 'storecupboard supper' with good-quality frozen vegetables.

Serves 4

340 g (12 oz) penne or other pasta shapes
170 g (6 oz) young asparagus
170 g (6 oz) green beans, trimmed and cut into 3 cm (1¼ in) lengths
170 g (6 oz) shelled fresh peas
1 tbsp extra virgin olive oil
1 onion, chopped
1 garlic clove, chopped
85 g (3 oz) pancetta, chopped
115 g (4 oz) button mushrooms, chopped
1 tbsp plain flour
240 ml (8 fl oz) dry white wine
4 tbsp single cream
2 tbsp chopped mixed fresh herbs, such as parsley and thyme
salt and pepper

Preparation time: 15 minutes
Cooking time: 15 minutes

Each serving provides

kcal 560, protein 20 g, fat 17 g (of which saturated fat 6 g), carbohydrate 77 g (of which sugars 5.5 g), fibre 7 g

✓✓✓	C
✓✓	B₁, folate, niacin, copper, iron
✓	A, potassium, selenium

1 Cook the pasta in boiling water for 10–12 minutes, or according to the packet instructions, until al dente. Drain well.

2 While the pasta is cooking, cut the asparagus into 3.5 cm (1½ in) lengths, keeping the tips separate. Drop the pieces of asparagus stalk, the green beans and peas into a saucepan of boiling water. Bring back to the boil and cook for 5 minutes. Add the asparagus tips and cook for a further 2 minutes. Drain thoroughly.

3 Heat the oil in a saucepan. Add the onion and cook for 3–4 minutes or until softened. Add the garlic, pancetta and mushrooms, and continue to cook, stirring occasionally, for a further 2 minutes.

4 Stir in the flour, then gradually pour in the wine and bring to the boil, stirring. Simmer until the sauce is thickened. Stir in the cream and herbs with seasoning to taste. Add the vegetables to the sauce and heat gently for 1–2 minutes, without boiling.

5 Divide the pasta among 4 serving bowls and spoon the sauce over the top. Serve immediately.

Some more ideas

● For a vegetarian version, omit the pancetta and add 170 g (6 oz) shelled young broad beans, cooking them with the asparagus stalks and the green beans. Once drained, the skins may be slipped off the broad beans, if preferred. Add 4 shredded fresh sage leaves with the parsley and thyme, or try tarragon for a slightly aniseed flavour.

● Omit the pancetta and instead serve sprinkled with freshly grated Parmesan cheese – about 45 g (1½ oz) in total for the 4 portions.

● Use frozen peas instead of fresh, adding them with the asparagus tips.

Plus points

● Asparagus is a good source of many of the B vitamins, especially folate, which is important during the early stages of pregnancy to help to prevent birth defects such as spina bifida.

● Peas provide good amounts of the B vitamins B₁, niacin and B₆. They also provide dietary fibre, particularly the soluble variety, some folate and vitamin C.

Tagliatelle with broccoli, cauliflower and blue cheese

This quick supper dish with a creamy sauce is so delicious that everyone will be surprised to learn that the sauce is made from only one ingredient. Colour and texture are provided by broccoli and cauliflower. Offer bread to complement the vegetables and a simple tomato salad to contrast with the creamy sauce.

Serves 2

170 g (6 oz) spinach tagliatelle
150 g (5½ oz) broccoli florets
150 g (5½ oz) cauliflower florets
200 g (7 oz) Cambazola (German blue brie cheese), rind removed, then diced
freshly grated nutmeg
salt and pepper

Preparation time: 10 minutes
Cooking time: about 15 minutes

1 Cook the tagliatelle in boiling water for 10–12 minutes, or according to the instructions on the packet, until al dente.

2 Meanwhile, cut the broccoli and cauliflower florets into bite-sized pieces. Add them to the simmering pasta for the last 2–3 minutes of the cooking time. Drain the pasta and vegetables in a large colander.

3 Return the rinsed-out pan to the hob and add the cheese. Turn the heat to the lowest setting and melt the cheese gently, stirring frequently to make a smooth sauce. As soon as the cheese has melted, add the cooked pasta and vegetables. Turn the pasta and vegetables in the cheese sauce to coat well and heat through. Season to taste with nutmeg, salt and black pepper, and serve immediately.

Plus points

● Broccoli and cauliflower belong to the cruciferous family of vegetables, all of which contain a number of phytochemicals, including indoles. Animal studies suggest that these phytochemicals may help to protect against breast cancer. Cruciferous vegetables also provide sulphoraphane which can stimulate the liver to produce cancer-fighting enzymes.

Some more ideas

● Add 100 g (3½ oz) carrots, cut into short, thin strips, with the other vegetables. Alternatively, replace either the cauliflower or the broccoli with 200 g (7 oz) carrots.
● For a peppery flavour, and a good source of iron, add 55 g (2 oz) roughly chopped watercress. Stir in the watercress when adding the pasta and vegetables to the melted cheese.
● Use ordinary brie or Camembert instead of the soft blue cheese, and add about 1 tbsp finely shredded fresh basil just before serving.
● For a stronger blue cheese flavour, choose Saint Agur or Gorgonzola.

Each serving provides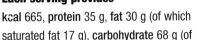

kcal 665, protein 35 g, fat 30 g (of which saturated fat 17 g), carbohydrate 68 g (of which sugars 5 g), fibre 6 g

✓✓✓ A, C, calcium

✓✓ B₁, B₂, B₆, B₁₂, folate, niacin, copper, iron, potassium, selenium

Creamy goat's cheese tagliatelle with toasted hazelnuts

When you are hungry and in a hurry this simple pasta dish can be on the table in next to no time. You will even be able to put together a salad accompaniment and still be sitting down to eat within 20 minutes. Take care when melting the cheese to ensure that it does not get too hot.

Serves 4

300 g (10½ oz) tagliatelle
90 ml (3 fl oz) semi-skimmed milk
150 g (5½ oz) medium-fat soft goat's cheese
2 tsp finely chopped fresh tarragon
6 spring onions, finely sliced
2–3 tbsp finely chopped toasted hazelnuts
salt and pepper

Preparation time: 5 minutes
Cooking time: 10–12 minutes

1 Cook the pasta in boiling water for 10–12 minutes, or according to the packet instructions, until al dente.

2 Meanwhile, warm the milk in a saucepan over a low heat. Add the cheese, breaking it up as you add it to the milk, and stir until it has just melted. Do not allow the mixture to boil or the cheese will curdle.

3 Remove from the heat and stir in the tarragon and spring onions. Season to taste.

4 Drain the pasta well and transfer it to a serving dish. Add the goat's cheese sauce and mix well. Scatter the hazelnuts over the top and serve.

Plus points

• Goat's cheese provides useful amounts of protein, the minerals calcium and phosphorus, and the B vitamins B_1, niacin, B_6 and B_{12}. Using medium-fat goat's cheese keeps the fat content of the recipe down: it contains about half the fat of Cheddar.

Some more ideas

• For an almost-instant supper, use fresh pasta (which cooks more quickly than dried) and 250 g (9 oz) reduced-fat garlic and herb soft cheese instead of the goat's cheese and spring onions. Mix a dash of milk with the soft cheese, then toss it with the hot pasta.

• Toast 4 tbsp coarse breadcrumbs under the grill until crisp and golden, and scatter them over the pasta as a lower-fat alternative to the toasted hazelnuts.

Each serving provides   Ⓥ

kcal 400, **protein** 16 g, **fat** 13 g (of which saturated fat 5 g), **carbohydrate** 60 g (of which sugars 4 g), **fibre** 3 g

✓✓ B_2, B_{12}, niacin, calcium

✓   A, E, copper, selenium

Hot conchiglie with grilled pepper and tomato dressing

Grilling green peppers gives them a slightly smoky taste and makes it easy to slip off their skins. They give a great flavour and vitamin boost to the diced tomato and Kalamata olive dressing in this speedy dish. Serve it for a light lunch or supper, with a simple green salad accompaniment.

Serves 4

3 green peppers

450 g (1 lb) ripe tomatoes

3 garlic cloves, finely chopped

1 tbsp red wine vinegar

1 tsp crushed dried red chillies (optional)

4 tbsp extra virgin olive oil

10 Kalamata or other black olives, stoned and halved

3 tbsp finely chopped fresh basil

3 tbsp finely chopped rocket

400 g (14 oz) conchiglie (pasta shells), or other shapes such as penne

salt and pepper

rocket leaves to garnish (optional)

Preparation time: 15 minutes
Cooking time: 10–12 minutes

1 Preheat the grill to high and grill the green peppers, turning occasionally, until the skin is blistered and blackened all over. Place the peppers in a polythene bag and leave until they are cool enough to handle and the skins are loosened.

2 Peel and seed the peppers, then cut them into bite-sized pieces. Cut the tomatoes into similar-sized pieces and mix them with the peppers. Add the garlic, wine vinegar, chilli flakes (if using), olive oil, olives, basil and rocket, and mix well. Set the dressing mixture aside to marinate while you cook the pasta.

3 Cook the pasta in boiling water for 10–12 minutes, or according to the packet instructions, until al dente. Drain and toss with the marinated pepper and tomato dressing. Garnish with rocket leaves, if liked, then serve immediately.

Plus points

● Green peppers are an excellent source of vitamin C, which is important for maintaining and healing the body's immune system. Even when grilled, useful amounts of the vitamin remain. Peppers also provide good amounts of vitamin A (through beta-carotene).

● Olives have a relatively high fat content, but most of it is the unsaturated type, which is believed to be the healthiest kind of fat to consume.

Another idea

● Add a can of chickpeas, about 400 g, drained, to the marinating peppers and tomatoes.

Each serving provides Ⓥ

kcal 490, **protein** 14 g, **fat** 14 g (of which saturated fat 2 g), **carbohydrate** 82 g (of which sugars 8.5 g), **fibre** 6 g

✓✓✓	C
✓✓	E, niacin, copper, selenium
✓	A, B$_1$, B$_6$, folate, iron, potassium

Everyday Pasta Power

Sustaining and wholesome for all the family

DAY-TO-DAY CATERING is as easy as can be with pasta-based meals. Pasta served in a hearty flat omelette, in a crispy oven-bake with turkey, or in a soufflé-topped dish with sweetcorn will appeal to all ages. You can update old favourites such as macaroni cheese and spaghetti bolognese by adding lots of vegetables, or try a chilli made with minced turkey and served with spaghetti. For hearty one-pot meals, add pasta to a beef or pork casserole. Or for something a little different, try pasta with spicy lentils or roasted vegetables and sunflower seeds.

Pasta frittata

Pasta is a convenient and delicious alternative to potato in flat omelettes, especially if you have some left over from a previous meal. This version, flavoured with ham and packed with vegetables, is complemented by a courgette and tomato salad. It makes a simple but satisfying lunch served with chunks of bread.

Serves 4

100 g (3½ oz) campanelle (pasta bells) or
    other shapes such as fusilli (spirals),
    or 225 g (8 oz) cooked pasta
2 tbsp extra virgin olive oil
1 large onion, finely chopped
2 garlic cloves, thinly sliced
1 large red pepper, seeded and chopped
100 g (3½ oz) smoked ham, diced
100 g (3½ oz) drained canned sweetcorn or
    frozen sweetcorn, thawed
6 green olives, stoned
6 large eggs

Tomato and courgette salad

2 courgettes, coarsely grated and squeezed to
    remove excess moisture
4 ripe tomatoes, roughly chopped
2 tbsp shredded fresh basil
2 tbsp lemon juice
salt and pepper

Preparation time: 10–20 minutes
Cooking time: 25 minutes

Each serving provides

kcal 365, **protein** 22.5 g, **fat** 19 g (of which
saturated fat 4 g), **carbohydrate** 29 g (of
which sugars 9 g), **fibre** 4 g

✓✓✓ A, B$_{12}$, C

✓✓   B$_1$, B$_2$, B$_6$, folate, niacin, iron

✓   E, copper, potassium, selenium

1 If necessary, cook the pasta in boiling water for 10–12 minutes, or according to the packet instructions, until al dente. Drain well.

2 Heat the oil in a large frying pan, add the onion and garlic and fry over a moderate heat until beginning to colour. Stir in the red pepper and fry for a further 5 minutes or until softened.

3 Stir in the ham, sweetcorn, olives and pasta, then spread out the ingredients to distribute them evenly in the pan. Beat the eggs with 3 tbsp water and seasoning to taste, and pour them into the pan.

4 Cook over a low heat for 8–10 minutes or until the omelette is almost set. Meanwhile, preheat the grill. Transfer the pan to the grill, placing it close to the heat. Grill for a few minutes to set the top.

5 While the omelette is cooking, make the salad. Stir the courgettes and tomatoes with the basil, lemon juice and seasoning to taste. (The lemon juice draws out moisture from the courgettes, so do not mix the salad until you are ready to eat it.)

6 Serve the frittata, cut into wedges, with the salad. Crusty bread is a good accompaniment.

Plus points

● Eggs are often served with high-fat accompaniments, such as buttered toast or fried bacon, but combining them with a high proportion of vegetables is a very good way to include them in a healthy, well-balanced diet. Eggs provide a good source of protein and contain useful amounts of vitamins A, B$_2$, B$_{12}$, E and niacin.

● Sweetcorn contributes useful amounts of fibre and vitamin A.

Some more ideas

● For a vegetarian version, replace the ham with 85 g (3 oz) frozen peas. Add the peas to the pan when frying the pepper to give them a chance to cook before adding the egg mixture. For a lightly curried vegetarian version, also omit the olives and add 1 tsp Madras curry paste to the beaten egg.

● Use shredded fresh coriander in the salad instead of basil.

everyday pasta power

Macaroni and mushroom cheese

Introduce vegetables to old favourites for up-to-the-minute healthy family meals. This well-loved pasta dish is delicious with mushrooms, peas and peppers added. Using a small amount of powerful Roquefort cheese ensures that the sauce is creamy and full flavoured, but not too high in fat.

Serves 4

225 g (8 oz) macaroni or rigatoni
170 g (6 oz) frozen peas
2 tbsp sunflower oil
1 red pepper, seeded and chopped
225 g (8 oz) mushrooms, quartered if large
30 g (1 oz) plain flour
600 ml (1 pint) semi-skimmed milk
1 tbsp Dijon mustard
55 g (2 oz) Roquefort cheese, chopped
salt and pepper

Topping

30 g (1 oz) mature Cheddar cheese, grated
55 g (2 oz) fresh wholemeal breadcrumbs

Preparation time: 30 minutes
Cooking time: 10–15 minutes

1 Preheat the oven to 220ºC (425ºF, gas mark 7). Cook the pasta in boiling water for 10–12 minutes, or according to the packet instructions, until almost al dente. Add the peas for the final 2 minutes of cooking. Drain the pasta and peas well.

2 Heat the oil in a heavy-based saucepan and cook the red pepper for 1–2 minutes. Add the mushrooms and cook for 2–3 minutes or until softened, stirring occasionally.

3 Stir in the flour, then gradually stir in the milk and bring to the boil, stirring. Simmer until thickened.

4 Add the mustard and Roquefort cheese with seasoning to taste (remember, though, that Roquefort is quite salty) and stir until the cheese has melted. Add the pasta and peas and mix in thoroughly. Pour the mixture into an ovenproof dish.

5 Mix the Cheddar cheese with the breadcrumbs and sprinkle this over the pasta mixture. Bake for 10–15 minutes or until lightly browned and bubbling hot. Serve immediately.

Plus points

- Frozen vegetables often contain more vitamin C than fresh vegetables. For example, frozen peas retain 60–70% of their vitamin C content after freezing and maintain this level throughout storage.
- Roquefort cheese is high in fat and salt, but it has such a strong flavour that a little goes a long way. It is a good source of protein, calcium and phosphorus, and it provides useful amounts of the B vitamins B_1, B_2, B_6 and niacin.

Some more ideas

- Instead of baking the macaroni cheese, place it under a moderately hot grill until bubbling and the topping is golden.
- Button Brussels sprouts are delicious with pasta in a blue cheese sauce. Cook 225 g (8 oz) sprouts in boiling water until just tender, then drain well and cut in half. Take care not to over-cook the sprouts – they are at their best while still slightly crunchy. Use instead of the mushrooms, adding the sprouts with the pasta.

Each serving provides Ⓥ

kcal 515, **protein** 22 g, **fat** 17 g (of which saturated fat 7 g), **carbohydrate** 73 g (of which sugars 13 g), **fibre** 6 g

✓✓✓	A, C, calcium, copper
✓✓	B_1, B_2, E, folate, niacin, potassium, selenium
✓	B_6, B_{12}, iron

Seafood lasagne

Packed with seafood and lots of vegetables, this lasagne is a superb vitamin-rich, nutritious meal. Choose vegetables that are fresh and in season – when fresh peas, asparagus and runner beans are past, try broccoli, kale and sautéed mushrooms. Serve with bread and a salad of interesting mixed leaves.

Serves 6

3 tbsp extra virgin olive oil
1 small bulb of fennel, diced
1 onion, chopped
4 garlic cloves, coarsely chopped, or to taste
2 tbsp coarsely chopped fresh parsley
¼–½ tsp fennel seeds
¼–½ tsp dried mixed Italian herbs
pinch of crushed dried chillies
125 g (4½ oz) prepared squid
125 g (4½ oz) salmon fillet, skinned and cut into chunks
125 g (4½ oz) raw tiger prawns, peeled
125 g (4½ oz) shellfish cocktail mix
150 ml (5 fl oz) dry white wine
150 ml (5 fl oz) fish or vegetable stock
grated zest of ½ lemon
2 bay leaves
1 carrot, roughly chopped
1 kg (2¼ lb) tomatoes, diced
5 runner beans, cut into bite-sized pieces
1 courgette, sliced or diced
250 g (9 oz) asparagus tips
170 g (6 oz) shelled fresh or frozen peas
400 g (14 oz) no-precook lasagne
250 g (9 oz) ricotta cheese
2 eggs, lightly beaten
85 g (3 oz) Parmesan cheese, freshly grated
freshly grated nutmeg
salt, pepper and cayenne

Preparation time: about 1½ hours
Cooking time: 30 minutes

1 Preheat the oven to 180ºC (350ºF, gas mark 4). Heat 2 tbsp of the oil in a large saucepan. Add the fennel, onion and half of the garlic. Cook for about 5 minutes or until the onion has softened, then add the parsley, fennel seeds, Italian herbs and chilli flakes. Cook for 1–2 minutes.

2 Add the squid and salmon, and cook for about 1 minute, then stir in the prawns and cocktail mix. Cook for only a moment – about 30 seconds – then use a draining spoon to transfer the seafood to a bowl and set aside.

3 Add the wine, stock, lemon zest, bay leaves and carrot to the juices remaining in the pan. Boil for 5 minutes, or until the liquid is reduced to about 100 ml (3½ fl oz). Stir in the tomatoes and continue to cook over a high heat for 3–4 minutes or until reduced to a well-flavoured sauce.

4 Add the runner beans and remaining garlic. Cover and cook for 10 minutes. Stir in the courgette and season to taste. Cover and cook for 5 minutes, then add the asparagus and peas. Cook, covered, for 5 minutes.

5 Lightly grease a deep 28 cm (11 in) lasagne dish with a little of the remaining oil. Place about two-thirds of the vegetables in the dish, lifting them out of the sauce with a slotted spoon and discarding the bay leaves, then top with a layer of lasagne, overlapping the sheets slightly. Add the seafood and a second layer of overlapping lasagne. Pour on the remaining vegetables and sauce. Top with the remaining sheets of lasagne.

6 Mix the ricotta cheese with the eggs and Parmesan. Season with a little nutmeg, salt, pepper and cayenne. Pour this evenly over the top of the lasagne and drizzle with the remaining olive oil.

7 Bake for 30 minutes, or until the lasagne is heated through and the top is speckled golden brown. Serve immediately.

Plus points

• Oily fish, such as salmon, is rich in omega-3 fatty acids, which are a type of polyunsaturated fat believed to help protect against coronary heart disease and strokes.
• The Mediterranean diet is thought to be healthier than the average diet in the UK. One of the reasons for this is the use of olive oil, a monounsaturated fat, rather than butter and other saturated fats.

Some more ideas

● When fresh tomatoes are lacking in flavour, add 1 tbsp tomato purée and a pinch of sugar to the sauce.

● For a vegetarian lasagne, omit the seafood and step 2 of the recipe. Increase the vegetables – use 10–12 runner beans and 3 courgettes – and add 1 can flageolet beans, about 400 g, well drained.

● Vary the vegetables according to availability. For example, leave out the runner beans and increase the peas to 250 g (9 oz); use 2 celery sticks instead of the bulb of fennel; replace the fresh tomatoes with 2 cans chopped tomatoes, about 400 g each.

● If you don't like squid, or any other of the fish and seafood ingredients listed, simply leave them out and increase another seafood item.

Each serving provides

kcal 595, **protein** 38 g, **fat** 22 g (of which saturated fat 8 g), **carbohydrate** 60 g (of which sugars 11 g), **fibre** 6 g

✓✓✓	A, B$_1$, B$_{12}$, C, calcium, copper
✓✓	E, folate, niacin, iron, potassium, selenium
✓	B$_2$

Chicken and ricotta cannelloni

Cannelloni tubes are often filled with rich beef or veal mixtures, but this lighter version uses chicken with fresh vegetables to make a deliciously satisfying dish. The cannelloni can be stuffed and assembled early in the day, and left in the fridge until you are ready to bake them. Serve with crusty bread and a green salad.

Serves 6

300 g (10½ oz) minced chicken

55 g (2 oz) red pepper, seeded and finely diced

55 g (2 oz) leek, finely chopped

55 g (2 oz) frozen peas

250 g (9 oz) ricotta cheese

55 g (2 oz) mascarpone cheese

1 egg

4 tbsp finely chopped fresh herbs, such as parsley, chives or basil, or a mixture

24 x 7.5 cm (3 in) no-precook cannelloni tubes, about 185 g (6½ oz) in total

salt and pepper

Sauce

900 ml (1½ pints) semi-skimmed milk

½ onion, studded with 4 cloves

1 bay leaf

pinch of freshly grated nutmeg

55 g (2 oz) plain flour

Topping

45 g (1½ oz) fine fresh wholemeal breadcrumbs

45 g (1½ oz) Parmesan cheese, freshly grated

Preparation time: 45–50 minutes

Cooking time: 35–40 minutes

1 To prepare the sauce, pour the milk into a heavy-based saucepan. Add the clove-studded onion, bay leaf, nutmeg and seasoning to taste. Bring to the boil, then remove from the heat, cover and set aside to cool completely. This allows time for the ingredients to flavour the milk.

2 While the milk is infusing, heat a non-stick frying pan over a moderately high heat, add the minced chicken and cook until it turns white and crumbly, stirring frequently. Set aside to cool slightly.

3 Put the diced red pepper, leek and frozen peas in a heatproof bowl, pour in enough boiling water to cover them and leave for 30 seconds. Drain the vegetables well in a sieve.

4 Beat the ricotta, mascarpone and egg together, then mix in the chicken, the drained vegetables and herbs. Season to taste.

5 Now return to making the sauce. Using a draining spoon, remove and discard the flavourings from the cool milk. Whisking constantly, sprinkle the flour into the milk. When all the flour is incorporated, return the pan to a moderate heat and bring the sauce to the boil, still whisking. Reduce the heat and simmer gently, whisking frequently, for about 3 minutes.

6 Preheat the oven to 200°C (400°F, gas mark 6). Spread a layer of sauce on the bottom of a 30 cm (12 in) square ovenproof dish.

7 Use a teaspoon and your finger to fill the cannelloni tubes with the chicken mixture. Arrange them in a single layer on the sauce in the dish. Spoon the remaining sauce over the top.

8 For the topping, mix together the breadcrumbs and the Parmesan cheese, and sprinkle this over the cannelloni. Bake for 35–40 minutes or until the topping is crisp and golden and the sauce bubbling hot. Leave to stand for 10 minutes before serving.

Plus points

• Adding vegetables to cannelloni fillings will 'stretch' a small quantity of protein food, such as chicken. Frozen vegetables are better than canned as vitamins are destroyed during the canning process; however, when fresh or frozen vegetables are not available, use canned types to contribute fibre, flavour and bulk. Interestingly, from research carried out by a well-known frozen food company, frozen vegetables are just as nutritious as fresh and, in many cases, they contain a higher level of vitamin C.

Some more ideas

- For a fat-free topping, omit the Parmesan cheese and breadcrumbs, and lay sliced skinned tomatoes over the sauce-coated cannelloni.
- Use 85 g (3 oz) finely chopped, well-trimmed Parma ham instead of the chicken, and replace the leek with 2 finely chopped spring onions. Increase the peas to 100 g (3½ oz).

- Replace the sauce with a classic béchamel (see page 24), made with 900 ml (1½ pints) milk and 85 g (3 oz) each butter and flour. The béchamel sauce will increase the fat content of the dish as well as the calories, but is delicious for a special occasion.

Each serving provides

kcal 445, **protein** 29 g, **fat** 18 g (of which saturated fat 10 g), **carbohydrate** 43 g (of which sugars 10 g), **fibre** 2 g

✓✓✓	A, calcium
✓✓	B₂, B₁₂, C, niacin
✓	B₁, B₆, copper, potassium, selenium

Turkey, pasta and leek crisp

This warming dish appeals to children and adults alike, so it makes an ideal family meal. It is a good example of an everyday dish in which vegetables, pasta and breadcrumbs extend a modest portion of a protein food, which, being turkey, means the dish is low in fat too. Serve with a salad, and a fruity pudding to follow.

Serves 4

2 carrots, sliced

400 g (14 oz) leeks, sliced

450 ml (15 fl oz) vegetable or chicken stock

300 ml (10 fl oz) white wine or additional stock

300 g (10½ oz) cavatelli (fluted pasta shells) or other shapes such as fusilli (spirals)

2 tbsp extra virgin olive oil

400 g (14 oz) turkey breast fillet, skin removed, then cut into thin strips

300 ml (10 fl oz) semi-skimmed milk

45 g (1½ oz) plain flour

salt and pepper

Topping

50 g (1¾ oz) fresh wholemeal breadcrumbs

2 tbsp grated Cheddar cheese

2 tbsp chopped fresh parsley

Preparation time: about 1 hour

Cooking time: 15 minutes

Each serving provides

kcal 635, **protein** 40 g, **fat** 14 g (of which saturated fat 4 g), **carbohydrate** 80 g (of which sugars 10 g), **fibre** 6.5 g

✓✓✓	A, B$_{12}$, C, niacin, calcium
✓✓	B$_1$, B$_6$, folate, copper, iron, potassium, selenium
✓	B$_2$

1 Place the carrots and leeks in a saucepan. Add the stock and the wine, if using, and bring to the boil. Reduce the heat, cover the pan and simmer for about 15 minutes or until the carrots are tender but not soft.

2 Drain the vegetables, reserving the stock. Place the vegetables in a large ovenproof dish. Return the stock to the pan and boil it until it is reduced to about 300 ml (10 fl oz). Set aside to cool.

3 Cook the pasta in boiling water for 10–12 minutes, or according to the packet instructions, until al dente. Drain well and add to the vegetables; mix together. Preheat the oven to 190°C (375°F, gas mark 5).

4 Heat the oil in a saucepan. Add the turkey and cook, stirring, for 5–10 minutes or until lightly browned. Use a draining spoon to remove the turkey from the pan and mix it with the pasta and vegetables.

5 Remove the pan from the heat and pour in the milk and cooled stock. Whisking constantly, sprinkle the flour into the liquid. Return the pan to the heat and bring the sauce to the boil, still whisking. Reduce the heat and simmer gently for 3 minutes, whisking frequently, until the sauce is thick and smooth. Add seasoning to taste.

6 Pour the sauce over the pasta mixture, coating it evenly. Mix together the breadcrumbs, cheese and parsley, and sprinkle this evenly over the top. Bake for about 15 minutes or until crisp and golden.

Some more ideas

• Use skinless boneless chicken breasts (fillets) instead of turkey, and spinach-flavoured pasta shapes.

• The leeks and carrots can be replaced by 450 g (1 lb) broccoli florets and 170 g (6 oz) button mushrooms. Simmer the broccoli for only 4–5 minutes; cook the mushrooms – sliced if large – with the turkey.

Plus points

• Turkey is one of the lowest-fat meats available, and most of the fat is in the skin, which is removed here.

• Being a starchy carbohydrate, pasta is an excellent energy-giving and satisfying food for all the family. The energy is slowly released as the pasta is digested, so helping to prevent between-meal hunger pangs.

Rigatoni with garlicky sausage

Aubergine can contribute succulent texture to pasta sauces. Here, the aubergine provides the perfect complement to tasty Toulouse sausage and olives, simmered with canned cherry tomatoes and fresh herbs. Tossed with chunky pasta, the result is a speedy well-balanced meal that tastes terrific.

Serves 4

300 g (10½ oz) rigatoni or other chunky pasta
  shapes, such as lumache (snails)

250 g (9 oz) Toulouse sausages

2 tbsp extra virgin olive oil

1 large red onion, roughly chopped

3 garlic cloves, crushed

1 aubergine, diced

3 small courgettes, diced

2 cans cherry tomatoes or chopped
  tomatoes, about 400 g each

2 tsp chopped fresh oregano

30 g (1 oz) black olives, stoned

3 tbsp chopped fresh flat-leaf parsley

salt and pepper

To serve

fresh oregano leaves

4 tbsp freshly grated Parmesan cheese
  (optional)

Preparation time: 15 minutes
Cooking time: 30 minutes

Each serving provides

kcal 640, **protein** 25 g, **fat** 28.5 g (of which
saturated fat 10 g), **carbohydrate** 75 g (of
which sugars 12 g), **fibre** 7 g

✓✓✓	calcium, copper
✓✓	A, B₁, B₆, C, E, niacin, iron, potassium, selenium
✓	folate

1 Cook the pasta shapes in boiling water for 10–12 minutes, or according to the packet instructions, until al dente. Drain well.

2 While the pasta is cooking, grill the Toulouse sausages until browned, turning once. Cool slightly, then cut them into chunky slices and set aside.

3 Heat the oil in a saucepan and fry the onion over a moderate heat for 2–3 minutes or until it begins to soften and colour. Add the garlic and sliced sausages, and continue to cook for a few minutes. Increase the heat, add the aubergine and courgettes, and cook, stirring, for 5 minutes or until the aubergine begins to soften.

4 Pour in one can of tomatoes, with the juice. Drain the juice from the second can into the pan (reserve the tomatoes), then stir in the oregano and seasoning to taste.

5 Cover and simmer gently, stirring occasionally, for 15 minutes or until the aubergine is tender. Add the olives and the reserved tomatoes and stir well. Cover the pan again and cook for a further 5 minutes.

6 Finally, mix in the pasta until it is thoroughly coated. Stir in the chopped parsley. Serve immediately, sprinkled with oregano leaves and Parmesan, if liked.

Plus points

● Aubergine is an ideal vegetable for adding bulk and fibre to a dish without adding calories.

● The oil derived from olives is high in monounsaturated fatty acids. These are thought to assist in lowering cholesterol levels in the blood.

Some more ideas

● Use prime-quality high-meat-content pork sausages, or turkey or chicken sausages, instead of Toulouse.

● For a vegetarian sauce, replace the sausages with chickpeas. Soak 100 g (3½ oz) dried chickpeas overnight, then cook them in boiling water for about 45 minutes or until tender. (Alternatively, use 1 can chickpeas, about 400 g, drained.) Add the chickpeas to the sauce at the last moment to ensure they keep their shape. Omit the oregano. Stir in 15 g (½ oz) rocket leaves instead of the parsley, and serve immediately before the rocket has time to wilt.

Spicy turkey chilli with spaghetti

Sweet peppers and warm spices flavour this family-style chilli, made with minced turkey rather than the traditional beef for a lower fat content, and served on spaghetti to boost the carbohydrate value. It is an ideal cook-ahead dish as the flavour of the sauce improves if it is made a day in advance and reheated.

Serves 4

1 tbsp sunflower oil

1 large garlic clove, crushed

1 onion, finely chopped

2 red or green peppers, seeded and finely chopped

1½ tsp cayenne pepper, or to taste

2 tsp ground cumin

1 tsp dried oregano

500 g (1 lb 2 oz) minced turkey

2 cans chopped tomatoes, about 400 g each

1 can red kidney beans, about 400 g, drained and rinsed

400 g (14 oz) spaghetti

salt and pepper

Topping

150 g (5½ oz) plain low-fat yogurt

1 spring onion, finely chopped

4 tbsp finely chopped mixed fresh herbs, such as parsley, coriander and chives

Preparation time: 10 minutes

Cooking time: about 25 minutes

Each serving provides

kcal 690, **protein** 51 g, **fat** 9 g (of which saturated fat 2 g), **carbohydrate** 108 g (of which sugars 22 g), **fibre** 12 g

✓✓✓	A, B$_{12}$, C, niacin, iron, copper
✓✓	B$_1$, B$_6$, folate, calcium, potassium, zinc
✓	B$_2$, E

1 First make the topping. Mix the yogurt with the spring onion and herbs. Cover and chill until required.

2 Heat the oil in a large frying pan or a saucepan. Add the garlic and fry, stirring, for 30 seconds. Add the onion and red or green peppers, and fry, stirring occasionally, for 5 minutes or until softened.

3 Stir in the cayenne pepper, ground cumin and oregano, and continue to cook, stirring occasionally, for about 2 minutes. Add the turkey and cook, stirring occasionally, until it is browned and crumbly.

4 Stir in the tomatoes and kidney beans, and add seasoning to taste. Bring to the boil, then reduce the heat and simmer for 15 minutes.

5 Meanwhile, cook the spaghetti in boiling water for 10–12 minutes, or according to the packet instructions, until al dente. Drain well.

6 Divide the spaghetti among 4 plates and spoon an equal amount of turkey chilli over each serving. Top with the herb-flavoured yogurt and serve.

Some more ideas

● For a vegetarian chilli, replace the turkey with 500 g (1 lb 2 oz) Quorn, either finely chopped or in chunks. Quorn, sold chilled and ready to cook, is a vegetable alternative to meat. Technically known as mycoprotein, it grows in a similar way to mushrooms. Quorn is low in fat and a good source of protein.

● To increase the fibre content of this dish, serve the chilli spooned over wholemeal spaghetti or noodles.

Plus points

● Turkey is a good source of zinc and many B vitamins, particularly B$_1$, B$_{12}$ and niacin (excellent source). It also provides iron.

● Red kidney beans are low in fat and rich in carbohydrate. They provide good amounts of vitamins B$_1$, niacin and B$_6$, and useful amounts of iron. They are also a good source of soluble fibre, which can help to reduce high cholesterol levels in the blood. When eaten with pasta, rice or other grains, kidney beans and other pulses supply good amounts of high-quality protein.

everyday pasta power

110

Spinach and turkey foldovers

Fresh lasagne, bought or home-made, can be used in a variety of ways, as this recipe illustrates. If making home-made pasta for this dish, try flavouring the dough with fresh coriander or oregano (see pages 19–20).

Serves 4

1 tbsp extra virgin olive oil
1 onion, finely chopped
2 celery sticks, finely chopped
340 g (12 oz) minced turkey
2 garlic cloves, chopped
1 tsp plain flour
3 tomatoes, skinned and chopped
1 tbsp chopped fresh oregano
8 sheets fresh lasagne, about 170 g (6 oz)
140 g (5 oz) fresh breadcrumbs
3 tbsp freshly grated Parmesan cheese
salt and pepper
sprigs of fresh flat-leaf parsley to garnish

Spinach sauce

1½ tsp extra virgin olive oil
1 garlic clove, chopped
170 g (6 oz) spinach, chopped
2 tbsp plain flour
360 ml (12 fl oz) semi-skimmed milk
freshly grated nutmeg

Preparation time: about 1 hour
Cooking time: 20–25 minutes

Each serving provides

kcal 500, protein 38 g, fat 15 g (of which saturated fat 5 g), carbohydrate 56 g (of which sugars 9.5 g), fibre 3 g

✓✓✓	B₁₂, niacin, calcium
✓✓	A, C, folate, copper, potassium, selenium, zinc
✓	B₁, B₂, B₆, E, iron

1 Preheat the oven to 200°C (400°F, gas mark 6). Heat the oil in a frying pan. Add the onion and celery, and cook for 5 minutes or until softened.

2 Add the turkey and garlic, and continue to cook, stirring to break up the turkey, for about 5 minutes or until it is white and crumbly. Stir in the flour, then add the tomatoes, oregano and seasoning to taste. Cook for about 10 minutes, stirring occasionally.

3 Meanwhile, cook the lasagne in boiling water for 3–5 minutes, or according to the packet instructions, until al dente, then drain and rinse under cold water. Drain on a tea-towel, in a single layer, and set aside. Stir about three-quarters of the breadcrumbs into the cooked turkey mixture and set aside. Reserve the remaining breadcrumbs.

4 For the spinach sauce, heat the oil in a small saucepan and cook the garlic for 1 minute. Add the spinach and stir-fry for 4 minutes or until wilted, then stir in the flour. Gradually pour in the milk, stirring constantly, and bring to the boil. Season with freshly grated nutmeg, salt and pepper.

5 Spread about half the spinach sauce in a shallow ovenproof dish. Lay a sheet of lasagne on the sauce. Place a spoonful of the turkey mixture in the middle of the lasagne, then fold the pasta over to enclose the meat filling.

Slide to one end of the dish. Repeat with the remaining sheets of lasagne and turkey, filling and folding them in the dish and overlapping them neatly.

6 Spoon the remaining spinach sauce over the pasta. Mix the reserved breadcrumbs with the Parmesan cheese, and sprinkle this over the top. Bake for 20–25 minutes or until the topping is crisp and golden. Garnish with flat-leaf parsley and serve immediately.

Another idea

• Replace the turkey with lentils. Cook 340 g (12 oz) green lentils in boiling water for about 35–40 minutes, or according to the packet instructions, until tender. Drain and add with the tomatoes. Use fresh savory instead of oregano, if available, and season the lentil mixture with 1 tbsp soy sauce.

Plus points

• This recipe is a perfect example of a delicious dish that is ideal for healthy eating. Turkey, one of the lowest-fat meats available, is served with a sauce containing vitamin-rich leafy green vegetables. In addition, milk and cheese add some calcium.

everyday pasta power

113

Spaghetti bolognese

Here's a new lower-fat version of one of the pasta classics, a full-flavoured meat sauce tossed with strands of spaghetti and served with Parmesan cheese. There's less beef than in traditional recipes, but low-fat chicken livers enrich the sauce. Serve with a spinach, tomato and onion salad and lots of bread.

Serves 4

2 tbsp extra virgin olive oil
1 large onion, finely chopped
1 large carrot, finely chopped
2 celery sticks, finely chopped
2 garlic cloves, crushed
8 sun-dried tomatoes, finely chopped
250 g (9 oz) extra-lean ground beef
125 g (4½ oz) chicken livers, finely
  chopped
240 ml (8 fl oz) red wine
1 can chopped tomatoes, about 400 g
1 beef stock cube
1 tsp fresh thyme or marjoram leaves or
  ½ tsp dried thyme or oregano
3 tbsp chopped fresh parsley
340 g (12 oz) spaghetti
30 g (1 oz) Parmesan cheese, freshly grated
salt and pepper

Preparation time: 20 minutes
Cooking time: 45 minutes

Each serving provides

kcal 630, **protein** 34 g, **fat** 21 g (of which saturated fat 5 g), **carbohydrate** 70 g (of which sugars 8 g), **fibre** 4 g

✓✓✓	A, B₂, B₁₂, folate, niacin, copper, iron
✓✓	B₁, C, E, calcium, potassium, zinc
✓	B₆

1 Heat the oil in a large saucepan, add the onion, carrot, celery, garlic and sun-dried tomatoes, and fry for 5–10 minutes, stirring frequently, until the vegetables start to brown.

2 Add the beef and chicken livers and fry, stirring, until the meat is browned. Pour in the wine and tomatoes with their juice, then crumble in the stock cube. Stir in the herbs and seasoning to taste. Cover the pan and simmer for 30 minutes, stirring occasionally.

3 Meanwhile, cook the spaghetti in boiling water for 10–12 minutes, or according to the packet instructions, until al dente.

4 Drain the spaghetti and mix it with the meat sauce, tossing until the strands are well coated. Sprinkle with Parmesan cheese and serve immediately.

Some more ideas

• To make a vegetarian sauce, double the quantities of carrots and celery, and replace the meat and livers with 200 g (7 oz) green lentils. Use a vegetable stock cube dissolved in 750 ml (1¼ pints) boiling water. Simmer the sauce for 40 minutes or until the lentils are tender and the liquid has been absorbed.

• Minced pork, chicken or turkey can be used instead of the beef.

• Quorn, a low-fat vegetable protein alternative to meat, can be used instead of the beef and chicken livers.

Plus points

• Chicken livers are a good source of the B vitamins, vitamin A, zinc and copper. They are one of the richest sources of iron – a 100 g (3½ oz) serving provides about half the recommended daily intake.

• Combining chicken livers with a selection of vegetable flavouring ingredients reduces the overall proportion of meat without compromising on flavour. The rich sauce provides ample coating for a hearty portion of pasta.

everyday pasta power

One-pot steak and pasta casserole

Slim pasta spirals called fusilli are delicious cooked in a casserole of beef and vegetables. The dried, uncooked pasta is added towards the end of the cooking time so that it retains its al dente texture while still absorbing the savoury flavours of the meat, vegetables and oregano in the rich stew.

Serves 4

1 tbsp extra virgin olive oil

340 g (12 oz) lean braising steak, cut into 1 cm (½ in) cubes

1 onion, chopped

1 can chopped tomatoes, about 400 g

2 tbsp tomato purée

2 garlic cloves, crushed

1 litre (1¾ pints) beef or vegetable stock

3 large carrots, sliced

4 celery sticks, sliced

1 small swede, about 400 g (14 oz), chopped

225 g (8 oz) fusilli (pasta spirals)

1 tbsp chopped fresh oregano or 1 tsp dried oregano

salt and pepper

Preparation time: 15 minutes
Cooking time: about 1½ hours

1 Heat the oil in a large flameproof casserole and add the beef. Brown the meat all over, stirring frequently. Use a draining spoon to remove the meat from the pan.

2 Add the onion to the casserole and cook for about 5 minutes, stirring often, until it is softened. Then add the tomatoes with their juice, the tomato purée, garlic and 600 ml (1 pint) of the stock. Stir well and bring to the boil.

3 Return the beef to the casserole. Add the carrots, celery and swede with seasoning to taste. Cover and simmer gently for 1 hour or until the meat is tender.

4 Add the pasta and oregano with the remaining stock. Bring to simmering point, then reduce the heat and cover the casserole. Cook for 20–25 minutes or until the pasta is tender. Serve immediately.

Plus points

● Beef is an excellent source of iron and zinc. Iron from red meat is far more easily absorbed by the body than iron from vegetable sources.

● Swede is a member of the cruciferous family of vegetables, all of which have an important role to play in cancer prevention.

● Adding pasta and starchy root vegetables to a meat casserole increases its fibre content as well as the carbohydrate.

Some more ideas

● For a Mediterranean flavour, replace the carrots and swede with 1 red pepper and 1 yellow or green pepper, seeded and chopped. Add the peppers with the onion. Also add 170 g (6 oz) button mushrooms with the pasta.

● Try venison steak instead of the beef, and use whole baby carrots and turnips instead of the sliced carrots and chopped swede.

Each serving provides

kcal 400, **protein** 27.5 g, **fat** 8.5 g (of which saturated fat 2 g), **carbohydrate** 57 g (of which sugars 14 g), **fibre** 6 g

✓✓✓	A, B₁₂, C, niacin
✓✓	B₁, B₆, copper, iron, potassium, zinc
✓	B₂, E, folate, calcium, selenium

Cidered pork with red cabbage

Long simmering makes this hearty stew perfect for cool autumn days, when apples and cabbage are at their best. Experiment with different types of apples – Cox's are sweet and winey, Granny Smith tart and tangy, Golden Delicious juicy and mild. This flavoursome stew is also superb served with couscous instead of pasta.

Serves 6

1 tbsp sunflower oil

500 g (1 lb 2 oz) lean boneless pork shoulder, cut into bite-sized chunks

2 onions, chopped

2 dessert apples, peeled, cored and diced

1 carrot, diced

2 tbsp raisins

500 ml (17 fl oz) cider

250 ml (8½ fl oz) pork or chicken stock

2 bay leaves

¼ tsp fresh thyme leaves, or to taste

pinch of ground cinnamon

pinch of ground allspice

12 ready-to-eat prunes, stoned

½ red cabbage, cut into bite-sized pieces

1 tbsp tomato purée

450 g (1 lb) orecchiette (little pasta ears) or conchiglie (shells)

2 tbsp chopped fresh parsley

salt and pepper

Preparation time: 20 minutes

Cooking time: 2¼–2½ hours

Each serving provides

kcal 525, **protein** 28 g, **fat** 9 g (of which saturated fat 2.5 g), **carbohydrate** 80 g (of which sugars 24 g), **fibre** 5.5 g

✓✓✓	B_1, B_{12}, niacin
✓✓	copper, iron, potassium, selenium
✓	B_2, B_6, zinc

1 Heat the oil in a heavy-based saucepan or flameproof casserole, add the chunks of pork and cook until they are starting to brown. Add the onions and continue to cook until the pork and onions are both lightly browned, stirring occasionally.

2 Stir in the apples, carrot, raisins, cider, stock, bay leaves, thyme, cinnamon and allspice. Bring to the boil, then reduce the heat and cover the pan. Cook over a very low heat for about 1 hour.

3 Mix in the prunes and red cabbage and cover the pan again. Continue to cook gently for 1 hour or until the meat is very tender.

4 Stir in the tomato purée. Leave to cook gently, covered, while you cook the pasta.

5 Cook the pasta in boiling water for 10–12 minutes, or according to the packet instructions, until al dente.

6 Drain the pasta, then divide among 6 bowls. Ladle the cidered pork over. Sprinkle with parsley and serve.

Plus points

- Over the last 20 years, farmers have been breeding leaner pigs, and pork now contains considerably less fat than it did in the past. It also contains higher levels of the 'good' polyunsaturated fats. The average fat content of lean pork is just 3.5%, much the same as skinned chicken breast.

- Pork is a good source of zinc and it provides useful amounts of iron, as well as vitamins from the B group, particularly B_1, B_6, B_{12} and niacin.

- Prunes provide useful amounts of potassium, iron and vitamin B_6. They are also a good source of dietary fibre and, independently of this, they are known to have a laxative effect which can help in treating constipation.

Another idea

- To make a chunky borscht, increase the stock to 1 litre (1¾ pints). Add 3–4 grated cooked beetroot, 1 tbsp sugar and the juice of 1 lemon with the cabbage. Taste for sweet-sour balance, adding a little extra lemon juice or sugar, and ladle the borscht over pasta shells in deep bowls. Serve with a dollop of plain low-fat yogurt on each portion, and a sprinkling of dill.

everyday pasta power

Spaghetti carbonara with roasted tomato salad

This version of an all-time favourite makes use of lower-fat dairy products and dry-cured ham instead of bacon to make a healthier dish with no compromise on flavour. To complete the meal, a salad suggestion is included as part of the recipe, but you can always make your favourite leafy accompaniment if you prefer.

Serves 4

340 g (12 oz) spaghetti

100 g (3½ oz) Parma ham or Serrano ham, trimmed of excess fat

3 eggs

5 tbsp single cream

3 tbsp ricotta cheese

4 tbsp freshly grated Parmesan cheese

salt and pepper

Roasted tomato salad

450 g (1 lb) cherry tomatoes or baby plum tomatoes, halved

2 garlic cloves, very thinly sliced

8 large sprigs of fresh basil, shredded

2 tsp extra virgin olive oil

mixed green salad leaves, such as frisée, rocket, watercress, Little Gem lettuce hearts and/or shredded Chinese leaves

1 red onion, thinly sliced

½ cucumber, thinly sliced

1 small bulb of fennel, halved and thinly sliced

Preparation time: 20 minutes

Cooking time: 15 minutes

1 Prepare the salad first. Preheat the oven to 220°C (425°F, gas mark 7). Place the tomatoes in a shallow ovenproof dish, cut sides up. Sprinkle with the garlic slices and basil. Season to taste and trickle the oil over. Roast for 10 minutes.

2 Mix the salad leaves in a serving dish. Add the onion, cucumber and fennel. When the tomatoes are done, spoon them, with all their hot juices, over the greens.

3 While the tomatoes are roasting, cook the spaghetti in boiling water for 10–12 minutes, or according to the packet instructions, until al dente.

4 Meanwhile, dry-fry the slices of ham in a very hot, heavy-based frying pan for 2–3 minutes or until just crisp. Remove and drain on kitchen paper, then crumble or snip into small pieces. Set aside.

5 Beat the eggs with the cream, then mix in the ricotta, half of the Parmesan and a little seasoning.

6 Drain the pasta. Return the empty pan to the heat and pour in the egg mixture. Heat for about 1 minute over a low heat, stirring constantly, then tip the drained pasta back into the pan.

7 Toss the spaghetti with the creamy egg, working quickly to coat the strands with the mixture. The heat of the pan and the hot pasta will lightly set the eggs to form a creamy sauce.

8 Serve immediately, sprinkled with the remaining Parmesan cheese and the ham, and accompanied by the roasted tomato salad.

Plus points

- Serving an interesting salad as an important part of a meal is a good way to avoid over-indulging in fatty foods.
- Pasta scores healthily low on the Glycaemic Index, which means that it breaks down slowly into glucose and glycogen in the body, providing long-lasting energy.

Each serving provides

kcal 570, **protein** 30 g, **fat** 20 g (of which saturated fat 8.5 g), **carbohydrate** 71 g (of which sugars 10 g), **fibre** 5 g

✓✓✓ A, B_1, B_{12}, niacin, calcium

✓✓ B_2, C, folate, copper, potassium, zinc

✓ B_6, E, selenium

Some more ideas

● For a meat-free version, briefly cook 8 finely shredded large sage leaves in 15 g (½ oz) butter in the empty pasta pan before adding the egg mixture.

● Instead of roasting the tomatoes for the salad, they can be grilled. Preheat the grill to high. Sprinkle the tomato halves with the garlic and oil, but not the basil, and grill for 5 minutes. Add the basil to the salad leaves.

● Reduced-fat crème fraîche or even low-fat quark can be used instead of cream. Both of these will contribute a slightly tangy flavour to the dish. They will also reduce the saturated fat content.

Herb-infused aubergine lasagne

Aubergines make delicious lasagne, but traditional methods usually involve slicing them and frying in copious quantities of oil. Here, they are cubed and simmered with flavouring ingredients to make a rich, zesty sauce.

Serves 4

2 tbsp extra virgin olive oil

1 tbsp fennel seeds (optional)

1 bay leaf

1 large onion, chopped

1 garlic clove, crushed

1 celery stick, diced

1 carrot, diced

100 g (3½ oz) mushrooms, roughly chopped

3 tbsp chopped fresh marjoram or 1 tbsp dried oregano

6 fresh sage leaves, shredded, or 1 tbsp dried sage

2 large aubergines, cut into 1 cm (½ in) cubes

grated zest of 1 lemon

2 cans chopped tomatoes, about 400 g each

12 sheets fresh lasagne, about 250 g (9 oz) in total (see page 19 for home-made pasta)

450 g (1 lb) cottage cheese

2 tbsp plain flour

1 egg

100 ml (3½ fl oz) semi-skimmed milk

a little freshly grated nutmeg

2 tbsp freshly grated Parmesan cheese

salt and pepper

Preparation time: about 1 hour, plus 10 minutes standing

Cooking time: 45 minutes

1 Heat the oil in a large saucepan. Add the fennel seeds, if using, and the bay leaf, and cook for a few seconds until they sizzle, pressing the bay leaf with the back of a spoon to bring out its aroma and flavour.

2 Add the onion, garlic, celery, carrot, mushrooms, marjoram or oregano, and sage. Cook, stirring frequently, for about 10 minutes or until the vegetables are softened slightly, but not browned.

3 Stir in the aubergines and lemon zest, mixing the pieces with the other vegetables so that they absorb the oil and cooking juices. Continue to cook for 5 minutes, stirring often.

4 Pour in the tomatoes with their juice and add seasoning to taste. Bring to the boil, then reduce the heat and simmer the aubergine mixture for 15 minutes. Preheat the oven to 180°C (350°F, gas mark 4).

5 While the sauce is simmering, cook the lasagne in boiling water for 3–5 minutes, or according to the packet instructions, until al dente. Drain well and lay out the pieces on a clean tea-towel, in a single layer, to dry.

6 Purée the cottage cheese with the flour and egg in a food processor or blender until smooth. Alternatively, press the cottage cheese through a fine sieve, then beat in the flour and egg.

Add the milk and process again briefly or stir it into the sieved mixture. Season to taste with nutmeg, salt and pepper.

7 Pour half the aubergine mixture into a large lasagne dish or other large oblong or square ovenproof dish. Discard the bay leaf as you do so. Cover with half the lasagne, then add the remaining aubergine mixture and top with the rest of the lasagne, overlapping the pieces neatly.

8 Pour the cottage cheese mixture over the lasagne to cover it completely. Sprinkle the Parmesan cheese evenly over the top. Bake the lasagne for about 45 minutes or until the topping is set and deep golden.

9 Leave the lasagne to stand for 10 minutes before serving. This allows time for the pasta and sauce to cool and 'set' slightly.

Each serving provides

kcal 485, **protein** 34 g, **fat** 17 g (of which saturated fat 6 g), **carbohydrate** 50 g (of which sugars 14 g), **fibre** 5 g

✓✓✓	copper
✓✓	A, B_{12}, C, niacin, calcium, potassium, selenium
✓	B_1, B_2, B_6, E, folate

Some more ideas

● To make a beef lasagne with only a modest proportion of meat, replace one of the aubergines with 225 g (8 oz) lean minced beef. Omit the fennel seeds, and brown the beef before adding the bay leaf, onion and other ingredients as in the main recipe.

● Ratatouille (braised peppers, aubergines, courgettes and tomatoes) makes an excellent lasagne filling. Use your favourite recipe, adding the quick cottage cheese topping instead of a traditional béchamel sauce.

Plus points

● Aubergines are a useful vegetable for making satisfying meals without a high calorie content. They contain just 15 kcal per 100 g (3½ oz).

● Puréed cottage cheese makes a creamy base for a delicious low-fat lasagne topping.

Soufflé-topped pasta bake

A topping lightened with whisked egg whites and finished with a sprinkling of Parmesan can make a simple pasta and vegetable bake very special. You can use a wide variety of vegetables with the pasta in this easy version of a soufflé. Serve with a vitamin-packed salad of chicory and watercress.

Serves 4

30 g (1 oz) dried porcini mushrooms

150 ml (5 fl oz) boiling water

115 g (4 oz) small pasta shapes, such as ditali (thimbles) or conchiglie (shells)

1 tbsp extra virgin olive oil

1 onion, chopped

2 garlic cloves, chopped

30 g (1 oz) plain flour

240 ml (8 fl oz) semi-skimmed milk

2 eggs, separated

2 tbsp chopped fresh parsley

1 can sweetcorn, about 340 g, drained

2 tbsp freshly grated Parmesan cheese

salt and pepper

Preparation time: 30 minutes

Cooking time: 25 minutes

1 Preheat the oven to 190°C (375°F, gas mark 5). Place the dried porcini mushrooms in a small bowl and pour in the boiling water. Cover and leave to soak for 15 minutes.

2 While the mushrooms are soaking, cook the pasta shapes in boiling water for 10–12 minutes, or according to the packet instructions, until al dente. Drain the pasta well.

3 Drain the mushrooms, reserving the liquid, and chop them finely. Heat the oil in a heavy-based saucepan and fry the onion, garlic and mushrooms for 4 minutes or until the onion is softened but not browned. Sprinkle over the flour and stir in well, then gradually pour in the milk, stirring. Bring to the boil, stirring constantly, and simmer until thickened. Add seasoning to taste.

4 Pour half the sauce into a bowl. Stir in the egg yolks and set aside. Add the reserved mushroom liquid to the sauce left in the pan, then stir in the cooked pasta, parsley and sweetcorn. Turn this mixture into a greased 1.4 litre (2½ pint) ovenproof dish.

5 Whisk the egg whites until they stand in stiff peaks. Stir 2 spoonfuls of the whisked whites into the sauce in the bowl to lighten it, then, using a large metal spoon, carefully fold in the remaining whites.

6 Spoon the egg white mixture over the pasta mixture and spread it out gently to the edge of the dish. Sprinkle with the Parmesan cheese and bake for 25 minutes or until puffed up and golden. Serve immediately, before the souffléed topping collapses.

Some more ideas

● Use 340 g (12 oz) small broccoli florets instead of the mushrooms and sweetcorn. Cook the broccoli florets in boiling water for about 3 minutes or until just tender. Drain, reserving 150 ml (5 fl oz) of the cooking liquid to use instead of the mushroom soaking liquid.

● Use wholemeal pasta shapes instead of plain.

Each serving provides Ⓥ

kcal 390, **protein** 16.5 g, **fat** 11 g (of which saturated fat 3.5 g), **carbohydrate** 60 g (of which sugars 13 g), **fibre** 2.5 g

---

✓✓ B_{12}, calcium

✓ A, B_1, B_2, niacin, iron, selenium

Plus points

● Sweetcorn provides useful amounts of fibre and vitamin A.

● Eggs are an inexpensive source of protein, and they contain useful amounts of vitamins A, E, B_2, B_{12} and niacin.

Noodles with roasted vegetables

Oven-roasted vegetables, tender and scented with garlic, make a chunky dressing that is great with wide pasta noodles. A sprinkling of crunchy sunflower seeds adds texture as well as additional nutritional benefits.

Serves 4

1 aubergine, cut into large chunks
2 courgettes, cut into large chunks
2 red peppers, quartered and seeded
1 green pepper, quartered and seeded
4 ripe tomatoes, halved
2 red onions, quartered
1 head garlic, cloves separated but unpeeled, plus 2 garlic cloves, chopped
3 tbsp extra virgin olive oil
cayenne pepper
50 g (1¾ oz) sunflower seeds
soy sauce
340 g (12 oz) wide pasta noodles, such as reginette, lasagnette or pappardelle
3 tbsp tomato purée, or to taste
handful of fresh basil leaves, coarsely chopped if large, or 2 tbsp chopped fresh parsley
salt and pepper

Preparation time: about 20 minutes
Cooking time: about 45 minutes

Each serving provides Ⓥ
kcal 530, **protein** 17 g, **fat** 17 g (of which saturated fat 2 g), **carbohydrate** 83 g (of which sugars 16 g), **fibre** 8.5 g

✓✓✓	A, C, E
✓✓	B₁, niacin, copper, potassium
✓	B₂, folate, iron

1 Preheat the oven to 190°C (375°F, gas mark 5). Arrange the aubergine, courgettes, red and green peppers, tomatoes, red onions and whole garlic cloves in a single layer in a large ovenproof dish or roasting tin. Sprinkle with about 2 tbsp of the olive oil, a little cayenne pepper, half the chopped garlic, and salt and pepper.

2 Roast for about 45 minutes or until the vegetables are tender but not soft and mushy, and are charred in places. Turn the vegetables once or twice during cooking, and increase the heat slightly if they are not cooking quickly enough.

3 Meanwhile, toast the sunflower seeds. Lightly brush a frying pan with just a few drops of olive oil, then heat the pan. Add the sunflower seeds and toss and turn them for a few moments until they begin to toast. Shake in a few drops of soy sauce and turn the seeds quickly, letting the soy sauce evaporate as the seeds toast and brown lightly. This should take about 4–5 minutes in total. Remove from the heat just before the seeds are crisp and leave them to cool in the pan. They will crisp up as they cool.

4 Cook the pasta in boiling water for 10–12 minutes, or according to the packet instructions, until al dente. Drain well and keep hot.

5 Using a knife and fork, cut the roasted vegetables into bite-sized chunks. Toss the vegetables and garlic with the remaining raw chopped garlic, the tomato purée and basil or parsley. Taste for seasoning.

6 Toss the pasta with the vegetables and serve immediately, sprinkled with the toasted sunflower seeds.

Some more ideas

• Crush a few saffron threads in a mortar using a pestle and add them to the roasted vegetables along with the tomato purée.
• Serve each portion of roasted vegetable pasta topped with a spoonful of low-fat fresh goat's cheese instead of toasted sunflower seeds.
• Pumpkin seeds can be used instead of sunflower seeds.

Plus points

• As well as all the benefits from the excellent mixture of vegetables in this dish, the sunflower seeds provide a useful source of iron, vitamin B₁ and phosphorus.

Leek and macaroni loaf with fresh tomato sauce

This is the perfect choice when you fancy a change from meat, and it will appeal to the whole family. For a well-balanced meal, start with a root vegetable soup, and serve the loaf with a mixed salad and crusty bread.

Serves 4

675 g (1½ lb) leeks

85 g (3 oz) macaroni or penne rigati (ridged penne)

1 tbsp extra virgin olive oil

30 g (1 oz) watercress

225 g (8 oz) cottage cheese, drained

55 g (2 oz) Parmesan cheese, freshly grated

3 eggs

1 medium-sized slice soft grain bread, about 30 g (1 oz)

2 tsp made English mustard

¼ tsp freshly grated nutmeg

salt and pepper

watercress sprigs to garnish

Tomato sauce

1 tbsp extra virgin olive oil

2 garlic cloves, crushed

500 g (1 lb 2 oz) ripe tomatoes, roughly chopped

6 fresh basil leaves

1 tbsp white wine vinegar

1 tsp sugar

Preparation time: 40 minutes, plus 10 minutes cooling

Cooking time: 1 hour

1 Preheat the oven to 180°C (350°F, gas mark 4). Carefully remove 6 outer layers from the leeks and reserve, then thinly slice the remainder.

2 Bring a large saucepan of water to the boil over a high heat. Cook the outer layers of leek for 3–4 minutes or until softened. Use a draining spoon to remove the leeks, and rinse them under cold water to cool. Set aside. Add the pasta to the pan, bring the water back to the boil and cook for 10–12 minutes, or according to the packet instructions, until al dente. Drain well.

3 While the pasta is cooking, heat the oil in a frying pan and stir-fry the sliced leeks over a high heat for 4–5 minutes or until all the liquid they yield has evaporated.

4 Purée the fried leeks with the watercress, cottage and Parmesan cheeses, eggs, bread, mustard, nutmeg and seasoning to taste in a food processor or blender. The mixture should be very smooth and creamy. Transfer the mixture to a bowl and stir in the drained pasta.

5 Grease a 1 kg (2¼ lb) loaf tin and line it with the strips of leek, overlapping them in the bottom and up the sides of the tin. Use 6 pieces for the main part of the tin and a piece for each end. Allow the excess leek to hang over the edges. Spoon the pasta mixture into the tin. Level the top and fold over the overhanging leeks.

6 Grease a piece of foil and use it to cover the tin, pinching it neatly around the edge. Half fill a roasting tin with boiling water, then stand the loaf tin in it. Bake for 1 hour or until the mixture is firm.

7 Meanwhile, to make the sauce, heat the oil in a small saucepan, stir in the garlic and cook for a few seconds. Add the tomatoes, basil, vinegar and sugar, and stir to mix. Cover and simmer for 10 minutes. Purée the sauce in a blender or food processor, then press it through a sieve to remove the seeds and skin. Season to taste.

8 Remove the loaf tin from the roasting tin of water and leave to stand for 10 minutes, to allow the loaf to set slightly before turning it out of the tin. Slice the loaf and serve the tomato sauce with it. Garnish with watercress.

Plus points

● Leeks are part of the onion family. They provide vitamin E as well as vitamin A from the carotene content of their green tops. If eaten regularly, leeks can help to reduce the chance of heart disease and stroke.

Some more ideas

● Replace the watercress and half of the Parmesan cheese with 3 chopped rashers of smoked back bacon. Fry the bacon in the oil and remove it from the pan before cooking the sliced leeks. Add the bacon to the mixture with the pasta. Garnish with fresh basil leaves.

● Cottage cheese with onion and chives can be used instead of plain cottage cheese.

Each serving provides

kcal 390, **protein** 26 g, **fat** 19 g (of which saturated fat 7 g), **carbohydrate** 31 g (of which sugars 11 g), **fibre** 6 g

✓✓✓ A, calcium

✓✓ B$_1$, B$_2$, B$_6$, B$_{12}$, C, E, niacin, copper, iron, potassium, selenium

Egyptian lentils with macaroni

For Egypt's vegetarians this highly spiced dish is a protein staple. On their own, lentils do not contain a lot of protein, but combined with the wheat in the pasta, they make a good protein dish that is low in fat.

Serves 4

250 g (9 oz) Puy lentils, rinsed

2½ tbsp sunflower oil

1 large onion, about 200 g (7 oz), very thinly sliced

sugar

1 large garlic clove, crushed

½ tsp turmeric

2 cans chopped tomatoes, about 400 g each

2 tsp ground cumin

2 tsp ground coriander

¼ tsp cayenne pepper

200 g (7 oz) macaroni

2 tbsp finely chopped fresh coriander or parsley

salt and pepper

Preparation time: 10–15 minutes

Cooking time: about 1 hour

Each serving provides ⓥ

kcal 460, **protein** 24 g, **fat** 8 g (of which saturated fat 0.9 g), **carbohydrate** 78 g (of which sugars 10 g), **fibre** 9 g

✓✓✓	copper, iron, selenium
✓✓	B₁, B₆, folate, niacin, potassium
✓	C, E, calcium

1 Put the lentils in a heavy-based saucepan and pour in enough water to cover them by 7.5 cm (3 in). Bring to the boil and boil vigorously for about 10 minutes, skimming the surface as necessary. Reduce the heat and simmer for 30–40 minutes or until tender. Drain well and keep warm.

2 Meanwhile, heat 1 tbsp of the oil in a large non-stick frying pan over a high heat. Add the onion and stir to coat with the oil, then reduce the heat and cook for about 20 minutes, stirring frequently, until soft. Stir in 1 tsp sugar, raise the heat and continue cooking, stirring, until the onion becomes dark brown and crisp. Immediately pour onto kitchen paper to drain, and set aside.

3 Heat ½ tbsp of the remaining oil in a large saucepan. Add the garlic and fry for 30 seconds, stirring. Stir in the turmeric and continue frying for a further 30 seconds. Pour in the tomatoes with their juice and add a pinch of sugar. Bring to the boil, stirring. Reduce the heat and simmer for 10–15 minutes, stirring occasionally, until the sauce thickens a little. Season to taste.

4 Heat the remaining oil in a frying pan. Stir in the cumin, ground coriander and cayenne pepper, and fry for about 30 seconds, stirring. Add the lentils and stir in seasoning to taste. Keep warm over a very low heat.

5 Cook the macaroni in boiling water for 10–12 minutes, or according to the packet instructions, until al dente. Drain well.

6 Spoon the macaroni onto a serving platter, and top with the spiced lentils and the tomato sauce. Sprinkle with the chopped coriander and top with the crisp onions. Serve at once.

Some more ideas

• Use red or green lentils instead of Puy lentils. Cook them according to the instructions on the packet.

• Add 1 seeded and thinly sliced red pepper to the lentil mixture, cooking it in the oil until slightly softened before adding the spices and cooked lentils.

Plus points

• Lentils are an excellent source of iron and of dietary fibre, particularly the soluble type. They also provide useful amounts of many B vitamins.

• The onion topping is traditionally deep fried, but here it is fried in a small amount of vegetable oil in a non-stick pan to reduce the fat content.

Gnocchi with sage and cinnamon

An Italian classic, traditional semolina gnocchi is served with generous amounts of cheese and butter. This healthier but equally delicious version is made with just a little butter, cheese and olive oil and flavoured with cinnamon and sage. Served with lightly cooked spinach and peas, this makes a great family meal.

Serves 4

750 ml (1¼ pints) semi-skimmed milk

150 g (5½ oz) semolina

1 tbsp chopped fresh sage or 1 tsp dried sage

¼ tsp ground cinnamon

30 g (1 oz) butter

1 large egg, beaten

55 g (2 oz) Parmesan cheese, freshly grated

2 tbsp extra virgin olive oil

salt and pepper

Pan-fried spinach with peas

1 tbsp extra virgin olive oil

2 garlic cloves, crushed

1 bunch of spring onions, chopped

150 g (5½ oz) frozen peas or petits pois

450 g (1 lb) spinach, shredded

lemon or lime wedges to garnish (optional)

Preparation time: 25 minutes, plus 5 minutes cooling

Cooking time: 20–25 minutes

Each serving provides Ⓥ

kcal 515, protein 23.5 g, fat 28 g (of which saturated fat 11 g), carbohydrate 44 g (of which sugars 13 g), fibre 5.5 g

✓✓✓	A, calcium, potassium
✓✓	B₂, B₁₂, C, folate, potassium
✓	B₁, B₆, E, copper, iron

1 Preheat the oven to 220ºC (425ºF, gas mark 7), and grease a Swiss roll tin or baking tray.

2 Bring the milk to the boil in a large non-stick or heavy-based saucepan. Remove from the heat and slowly sprinkle in the semolina while stirring constantly. Return the pan to the heat. Add the sage, cinnamon and seasoning to taste, then stir until the mixture boils. Reduce the heat and simmer, stirring, for a further 1–2 minutes or until the mixture is very thick.

3 Remove the pan from the heat and beat in the butter, then allow the mixture to cool slightly. Beat in the egg and three-quarters of the Parmesan cheese until thoroughly combined.

4 Pile the mixture onto the greased tin and use a wet spatula to spread it out into an oblong or square with a thickness of 1 cm (½ in). Leave to cool for about 5 minutes. Then cut the mixture into 5 cm (2 in) squares.

5 Brush an ovenproof dish with a little of the oil and overlap the squares of gnocchi in it in a single layer. Trickle the remaining oil over and sprinkle with the remaining Parmesan. Bake for 20–25 minutes or until the gnocchi is golden and crisp on top. Prepare the pan-fried spinach just before the gnocchi is ready.

6 Heat the oil in a large saucepan. Add the garlic and spring onions, and cook for 1 minute. Stir in the frozen peas or petits pois and cook, stirring, for 2–3 minutes or until the peas are well thawed. Stir in the spinach and season to taste. Cook, stirring, for 2–3 minutes or until the peas are hot and the spinach has just wilted.

7 Serve immediately, garnishing the spinach and peas with lemon or lime wedges, if using, so that the juice can be added to taste.

Some more ideas

● Serve fresh tomato sauce with the gnocchi (see page 22).

● Use a round pastry cutter to cut the gnocchi into circles, and interleave thin slices of mozzarella cheese between the overlapping pieces before baking.

● Interleave the gnocchi with sliced tomatoes and mozzarella cheese on a bed of grilled sliced courgettes and aubergines, and then bake.

Plus points

● Semolina, milled from wheat grain, is a starchy carbohydrate that also provides some protein as well as manganese and phosphorus.

Especially Good

Extra-special pasta fit for dinner party fare

WHEN YOU WANT TO PREPARE something especially good to eat yet healthy too, a pasta dish is an ideal choice. You could begin with little stuffed Oriental dumplings, or perhaps a pretty rotolo filled with spinach and ricotta and served with red pepper sauce. For a meaty main dish, you might choose penne with a zesty mixture of duck, rhubarb and orange, or low-fat venison meatballs in a rich red wine sauce with spaghetti. Seafood with spaghettini is an elegant dish, as is tagliatelle with mushrooms and Marsala. And if you really want to impress your guests, try serving stuffed giant pasta shells baked in a creamy Parmesan and walnut sauce, or make your own ravioli.

Spaghettini with seafood

Cooked in a delicious wine-enriched tomato sauce, a nutritious mix of seafood makes an elegant partner for the long thin pasta called spaghettini. Prepare a leafy mixed side salad with a wide variety of attractive and flavoursome greenery to go with this dinner party main course.

Serves 4

2 tbsp extra virgin olive oil

1 onion, chopped

2–3 garlic cloves, chopped

2 tbsp chopped fresh parsley

250 ml (8½ fl oz) dry white wine

1 can chopped tomatoes, about 400 g

pinch of crushed dried chillies

¼ tsp sugar

pinch of saffron threads

8–12 mussels, scrubbed and beards removed

2 squid, cleaned, then tentacles cut into bite-sized pieces and bodies cut into rings

300 g (10½ oz) raw tiger or king prawns, peeled

400 g (14 oz) spaghettini

salt and pepper

sprigs of fresh oregano or marjoram to garnish

Preparation time: 25 minutes

Cooking time: about 45 minutes

Each serving provides

kcal 580, **protein** 39 g, **fat** 10 g (of which saturated fat 1.5 g), **carbohydrate** 80 g (of which sugars 8 g), **fibre** 4 g

✓✓✓	B_{12}, copper
✓✓	B_6, E, niacin, calcium, potassium, selenium
✓	B_1, C

1 Heat the oil in a large saucepan, add the onion and sauté for 5–7 minutes or until softened but not browned. Add the garlic and parsley and cook for a further 1 minute.

2 Pour in the wine and bring to the boil. Regulate the heat so that the wine boils steadily, and cook for about 15 minutes or until the wine has almost all evaporated.

3 Stir in the tomatoes with their juice, the crushed chillies, sugar and saffron. Reduce the heat and cook gently for 15 minutes. Season to taste.

4 Add the mussels. Cover and cook over a moderate heat for about 5 minutes or until the mussels start to open. Add the squid and prawns, and cook for a further 3–4 minutes or until the prawns turn from blue-grey to pink. Remove from the heat. Discard any mussels that have not opened, then cover the pan to retain the heat.

5 Meanwhile, cook the spaghettini in boiling water for 10 minutes, or according to the packet instructions, until al dente. Drain and return to the empty pan. Add some of the tomato sauce and toss the pasta until coated.

6 Serve the pasta with the remaining tomato sauce and seafood piled on top, garnished with small sprigs of fresh oregano or marjoram.

Plus points

• Shellfish contain useful amounts of B vitamins, particularly B_{12}, and they are a good source of the antioxidant selenium.

• Pasta and seafood make a delicious dish that is both special and nutritious: it is high in starchy carbohydrate and low in fat. Wine and tomatoes make a sauce that is far lower in fat than the usual cream-based dressings.

• Onions and garlic contain allicin, which has anti-fungal and antibiotic properties.

Some more ideas

• When tomatoes are in season, use 1 kg (2¼ lb) ripe plum tomatoes, peeled and diced, instead of canned. The cooking time for the sauce will be about 5 minutes longer. (You may need a little more sugar to balance the tangy flavour of fresh tomatoes.)

• Omit the squid and replace it with 200 g (7 oz) cooked or canned, drained cannellini beans. This will make a more substantial dish – high-fibre foods such as pulses are very filling – so you might want to reduce the quantity of pasta to 340 g (12 oz).

especially good

Mushroom ravioli in herb jus

Bought stuffed pasta just does not taste anything like silken-textured home-made pasta with a freshly prepared savoury filling. This is not a convenience meal – making pasta does take time – but the result is a marvellous dish, to savour and enjoy at a weekend. Fresh fruit will complete the meal.

Serves 6

3 tbsp extra virgin olive oil

4 shallots, chopped

1 garlic clove, chopped

450 g (1 lb) mushrooms, finely chopped

3 tbsp brandy

30 g (1 oz) dried porcini mushrooms, soaked, drained and finely chopped

100 g (3½ oz) fresh wholemeal breadcrumbs

55 g (2 oz) Parmesan cheese, freshly grated

2 eggs

2 tbsp chopped fresh parsley or basil

1 tsp chopped fresh marjoram or ¼ tsp dried marjoram

1 quantity fresh pasta dough (see page 19)

250 g (9 oz) mange-tout or sugarsnap peas

2 tbsp tiny tender sprigs of fresh thyme

1 tbsp extra virgin olive oil (optional)

salt and pepper

Herb and garlic jus

750 ml (1¼ pints) chicken or vegetable stock

175 ml (6 fl oz) dry white wine

1 garlic clove, chopped

1 tbsp fresh thyme leaves or ¼ tsp dried thyme

4 courgettes, thinly sliced or coarsely diced

Preparation time: about 1 hour

Cooking time: 35–40 minutes

1 Heat the olive oil in a large saucepan. Add the shallots and cook for a few seconds, then add the garlic and the mushrooms. Cook over a high heat, stirring, to brown the mushrooms, then reduce the heat and cook for about 10 minutes or until the mixture has reduced in volume.

2 Pour in the brandy and cook, stirring, until it has evaporated. Remove from the heat and add seasoning to taste.

3 Stir in the porcini mushrooms, breadcrumbs, Parmesan, eggs, parsley or basil and marjoram. The ingredients should be thoroughly bound into a moist paste. Set aside in the fridge while you prepare the pasta.

4 Cut the pasta dough into quarters and roll out each separately. If using a pasta machine to roll the dough, use the second thinnest setting. Otherwise, roll it out by hand on an unfloured surface. Cut each rolled-out quarter into 2 strips, each about 10 x 50 cm (4 x 20 in).

5 Lay a pasta strip on the work surface. Dot the filling on the dough in small mounds (about 1 tsp each), about 5 cm (2 in) apart. Ensure that there is enough room between the mounds of filling for the covering of dough to stick to the base.

6 Brush the dough around each mound with a little water. Top with a second strip of pasta and press it down firmly around the filling to seal. Cut between the mounds of filling with a fluted pastry wheel or sharp knife.

7 Carefully pull the ravioli apart and toss with flour. Place in a single layer on a plate in the fridge. Repeat with the remaining dough and filling.

8 To make the herb and garlic jus, combine the stock, wine and garlic in a saucepan. Bring to the boil and cook over a high heat for 5–10 minutes or until the liquid is well flavoured. Add the thyme and courgettes, and continue cooking over a moderately high heat for 5–10 minutes or until the courgettes are quite tender but not mushy, and the liquid has intensified in flavour and evaporated slightly.

9 Meanwhile, cook the ravioli in boiling water for 4–5 minutes or until they rise to the surface and are al dente. Add the mange-tout or sugarsnap peas for the final 30–60 seconds of cooking. Drain well.

10 Serve the ravioli and mange-tout or sugarsnap peas in shallow soup bowls with the courgettes and jus ladled over. Sprinkle thyme over the top and drizzle with a tiny amount of olive oil, if using. Serve immediately.

especially good

Plus points

● Mushrooms are low in fat and calories, and they provide useful amounts of copper as well as some of the B vitamins.
● Mange-tout and sugarsnap peas are good sources of both vitamin C and fibre.

Some more ideas

● Flavour the fresh pasta dough with sun-dried tomato paste or black olive paste (see page 20).
● Bought wonton wrappers can be used instead of home-made pasta dough to make ravioli. Alternatively, buy fresh lasagne and roll it out slightly thinner, if necessary, then use it to make the ravioli.

Each serving provides

kcal 573, **protein** 25 g, **fat** 18 g (of which saturated fat 5 g), **carbohydrate** 70 g (of which sugars 5 g), **fibre** 6 g

✓✓✓	calcium, copper
✓✓	A, B₁₂, C, folate, niacin, potassium, selenium
✓	B₁, B₂, B₆, E

Zesty ginger duck with rhubarb

A full-flavoured, bitter-sweet mixture of duck with rhubarb and orange makes a tasty dressing for penne or rigatoni, showing that a modest portion of meat goes a long way with the right pasta in an interesting sauce. Crisp green vegetables complete this simple, but stylish, stir-fry.

Serves 4

340 g (12 oz) boneless duck breasts

400 g (14 oz) penne or other pasta shapes

1½ tbsp sunflower oil

1 large garlic clove, crushed

2 tbsp finely chopped fresh root ginger

225 g (8 oz) rhubarb, cut into 5 mm (¼ in) slices

10 spring onions, thinly sliced

300 g (10½ oz) runner or French beans, thinly sliced or cut into short lengths

75 g (2½ oz) watercress sprigs

4 oranges, peeled, halved and sliced

salt and pepper

Marinade

finely grated zest and juice of 1 large orange

3 tbsp sugar

1 tbsp soy sauce

1½ tsp finely chopped fresh root ginger

8 juniper berries, lightly crushed

4 black peppercorns, lightly crushed

Preparation time: 30 minutes, plus at least 30 minutes marinating

Cooking time: about 15 minutes

1 Place all the marinade ingredients in a saucepan and bring to the boil, stirring to dissolve the sugar. Pour the marinade into a bowl and set aside to cool while you prepare the duck breasts.

2 Remove the skin and all surface fat from the duck breasts. Thinly slice the breasts crossways, then cut the slices lengthways into fine strips. Add the strips to the marinade and stir to coat them well. Cover tightly and leave to marinate in a cool place, stirring occasionally, for at least 30 minutes.

3 When you are ready to prepare the stir-fry, cook the pasta in boiling water for 10–12 minutes, or according to the packet instructions, until al dente. Drain the pasta well and return it to the hot empty pan. Cover and set aside, off the heat.

4 Drain the duck in a sieve set over a bowl, pressing out all the liquid and reserving it. Heat a wok or large frying pan over a high heat. Add the oil and, when it is hot, cook the garlic and ginger for 30 seconds. Add the duck and stir-fry for 3–4 minutes or until the duck strips are well browned.

5 Add the rhubarb and spring onions. Reduce the heat to moderate and stir-fry for about 2 minutes or until the rhubarb is soft and tender but not broken down completely.

6 Pour in the reserved marinade and bring to the boil, stirring for a few seconds. Season with salt and pepper to taste, and remove from the heat. Add to the pasta and toss well. Keep hot.

7 Drop the beans into a saucepan of boiling water and cook for just 2 minutes. Drain well and rinse briefly with cold water.

8 Arrange the watercress on a large dish or on individual serving plates, and top with the hot beans and sliced oranges. Divide the duck and pasta mixture among the plates and serve.

Plus points

• Skinning the duck and removing the fat before cooking cuts out about two-thirds of the total fat content.

• Duck is a good source of many of the B vitamins, plus iron and zinc. Weight for weight, duck contains over twice as much B_1 and B_2, and three times as much iron, as chicken.

• Rhubarb contains vitamin C, manganese and potassium. Use only the stalks, however, because the leaves are poisonous, even when they are cooked.

especially good

Some more ideas

- Use 340 g (12 oz) lean boneless pork such as fillet instead of the duck breast.
- Try a combination of lean gammon instead of duck, and shelled broad beans instead of runner or French beans.
- When fresh rhubarb is out of season, use plums, stoned and sliced, instead.

- Nectarines, stoned and sliced, are a good alternative to rhubarb, particularly if you want to vary the dish by using lower-fat chicken or turkey breast instead of duck.

Each serving provides

kcal 580, **protein** 32 g, **fat** 11.5 g (of which saturated fat 2.4 g), **carbohydrate** 92.6 g (of which sugars 18 g), **fibre** 8.5 g

✓✓✓	C, copper
✓✓	B_{12}, potassium, selenium, zinc
✓	B_1, B_2, folate, niacin, calcium, iron

Pork pot-stickers with crisp and spicy peanut salad

These fragrant Chinese-style pasta purses are made with wonton wrappers, available from Oriental supermarkets. They are part fried, then simmered in stock and served on a bed of green leaves with a salad of crunchy vegetables, peanuts and coriander. Serve as an unusual first course for a Chinese feast.

Makes 20, to serve 4

250 g (9 oz) lean minced pork
55 g (2 oz) drained canned water chestnuts, finely chopped
3 spring onions, finely chopped
1 tbsp finely grated fresh root ginger
2 tbsp hoisin sauce
1 tbsp dark soy sauce
20 wonton wrappers
1 egg, beaten
2 tbsp sunflower oil
300 ml (10 fl oz) hot pork or chicken stock

Spicy peanut salad

7.5 cm (3 in) piece cucumber, seeded and finely diced
1 large carrot, finely diced
2 shallots, finely chopped
2–3 tbsp chopped fresh coriander
2 tbsp Thai dipping sauce for dim sum, or to taste
4 tbsp finely chopped salted peanuts
salt and pepper

To serve

4–8 crisp green leaves (such as Chinese leaves, iceberg or cos lettuce), torn into pieces if very large
sprigs of fresh coriander (optional)

Preparation time: 25 minutes
Cooking time: 15 minutes

1 Tip the pork into a bowl and mix in the water chestnuts, spring onions, ginger, hoisin sauce and soy sauce. (The easiest way to do this is with your hands.) Divide the mixture into 20 equal portions.

2 Brush a wonton wrapper with beaten egg and place a portion of the pork mixture in the centre. Gather up the wrapper around the pork and squeeze it together at the top to seal in the filling and form an old-fashioned moneybag shape. Repeat with the remaining pork and wonton wrappers.

3 Heat the oil in a large frying pan. Stand the pot-stickers in the pan, in one layer, cover and cook them very gently for 5 minutes or until they are lightly browned on the base.

4 Pour in enough hot stock to come halfway up the sides of the pot-stickers, then cover the pan again and simmer gently for 10 minutes or until the pasta is cooked.

5 Meanwhile, stir the vegetables and coriander together for the salad. Gradually add the dipping sauce, tasting the mixture to ensure that it is not too spicy for you, then add the peanuts and seasoning to taste.

6 To serve, arrange the crisp leaves on 4 large plates and pile 5 drained pot-stickers on top of each. Spoon some of the spicy peanut salad around the pot-stickers and garnish with coriander sprigs, if liked. Serve any remaining salad separately.

Plus points

• Peanuts are a good source of protein, niacin, phosphorus and potassium. Although they contain large amounts of fat, the majority of it is monounsaturated.

Each serving provides

kcal 300, **protein** 20.5 g, **fat** 20 g (of which saturated fat 4 g), **carbohydrate** 9 g (of which sugars 3 g), **fibre** 2 g

✓✓	A, B$_1$, B$_{12}$, niacin, copper
✓	E, iron, potassium, selenium

especially good

Some more ideas

● Instead of frying and then simmering the pot-stickers, they can be steamed as for dim sum with dipping sauce (see page 46). If you do not want to steam them on a bed of leaves, line the bottom of the steamer with foil, grease it with a little sunflower oil and then prick it all over to allow the steam to come through.

● For an alternative filling, replace the minced pork, hoisin sauce and water chestnuts with minced turkey, yellow bean stir-fry sauce and canned bamboo shoots.

● If you cannot find wonton wrappers, make your own dough following the instructions in 'Some more ideas' on page 46. Make a half quantity of dough for these pot-stickers.

Spaghetti with venison meatballs

A rich combination of red wine and venison brings a luxurious, low-fat twist to the ever-popular dish of spaghetti and meatballs. This goes down well at family gatherings and informal dinner parties.

Serves 4

500 g (1 lb 2 oz) minced venison

1 small onion, finely chopped

1 egg

3 tbsp plain flour

1 tbsp chopped fresh mixed herbs, such as thyme and parsley

2 tbsp extra virgin olive oil

340 g (12 oz) spaghetti

salt and pepper

shredded fresh basil to garnish

Red wine sauce

1 small onion, chopped

1 small red pepper, seeded and chopped

55 g (2 oz) mushrooms, chopped

1 celery stick, chopped

1 large garlic clove, crushed

300 ml (10 fl oz) red wine

200 ml (7 fl oz) beef stock

1 can chopped tomatoes, about 400 g

1 bouquet garni

Preparation time: 25 minutes

Cooking time: 40 minutes

Each serving provides

kcal 650, **protein** 41.5 g, **fat** 15 g (of which saturated fat 4 g), **carbohydrate** 80 g (of which sugars 10 g), **fibre** 5 g

✓✓✓	copper, iron
✓✓	A, B₆, B₁₂, C, niacin, potassium, zinc
✓	B₁, B₂, E, folate

1 Mix together the venison, chopped onion, egg, flour and herbs until well combined. Season with salt and pepper. Divide the mixture into 28 portions. Lightly flour your hands, then roll the portions into neat balls.

2 Heat the olive oil in a large non-stick frying pan or flameproof casserole and fry the meatballs, rolling them gently from time to time, for 8–10 minutes or until they are browned all over. (Brown the meatballs in batches, if necessary.) Use a draining spoon to remove the meatballs from the pan and set them aside.

3 For the sauce, add the onion, red pepper, mushrooms, celery and garlic to the juices in the frying pan and cook for 3 minutes, stirring frequently. Pour in the red wine and bring to the boil, then reduce the heat slightly and simmer for about 5 minutes or until the liquid has reduced by half.

4 Add the stock, tomatoes with their juice, and the bouquet garni to the pan and bring back to the boil. Reduce the heat and simmer for 10 minutes.

5 Return the meatballs to the pan and turn them over in the sauce. Simmer gently for 10 minutes.

6 Meanwhile, cook the spaghetti in boiling water for 10–12 minutes, or according to the packet instructions, until al dente. Drain well.

7 Taste the sauce and adjust the seasoning if necessary. Discard the bouquet garni. Divide the spaghetti among 4 serving plates or bowls and top with the meatballs and sauce. Garnish with shredded basil and serve immediately.

Some more ideas

• Use minced turkey instead of minced venison in the meatballs, and dry white wine instead of red wine in the sauce.

• Lean minced beef or pork, or a combination of the two, can be used instead of venison.

• Serve spinach tagliatelle or a combination of green and white *paglia e fieno* (mixed spinach and egg noodles) instead of spaghetti.

Plus points

• Venison is a good alternative to beef: it is exceptionally low in fat compared to other red meats, but still provides useful amounts of iron and B vitamins. Venison contains slightly less fat than uncooked skinless chicken breast – 1.1 g fat per 100 g (3½ oz) compared to 1.6 g fat.

especially good

Pappardelle with rabbit ragoût

Rabbit, a low-fat meat with a delicate flavour, is the classic ingredient for this Tuscan dish, although wild hare is often used. Pappardelle is its perfect pasta partner. Serve it with a radicchio salad, or combine mixed leaves, herbs, cucumber, courgette and green pepper to boost the vegetable content of the meal.

Serves 4

2½ tbsp extra virgin olive oil

2 onions, chopped

1 small bulb of fennel or 1 celery stick, diced

3 garlic cloves, chopped

55 g (2 oz) pancetta (about 3 slices), cut into
    small pieces

1 tbsp juniper berries, coarsely crushed

1 tbsp chopped fresh rosemary or 2 tsp dried
    rosemary

340 g (12 oz) boneless rabbit, cut into large
    chunks, or 500 g (1 lb 2 oz) rabbit joints

250 ml (8½ fl oz) red wine

400–450 ml (14–15 fl oz) chicken stock

3 tbsp tomato purée

340 g (12 oz) pappardelle or other wide flat
    noodles

75 g (2½ oz) Parmesan cheese, freshly
    grated, to serve

Preparation time: 20–25 minutes
Cooking time: 1–1¼ hours

Each serving provides

kcal 670, protein 40.5 g, fat 22 g (of which
saturated fat 8 g), carbohydrate 71 g (of
which sugars 7 g), fibre 5 g

✓✓✓	B₁₂, niacin, calcium
✓✓	copper, iron, potassium, selenium
✓	B₁, B₂, B₆

1 Heat 2 tbsp of the olive oil in a heavy-based saucepan or flameproof casserole. Add the onions, fennel or celery, garlic and pancetta, and cook for about 8 minutes, stirring occasionally, until the onions are softened but not browned.

2 Add the juniper berries, rosemary and rabbit. Cook over a fairly low heat until the rabbit pieces are lightly browned; this takes about 5 minutes.

3 Pour in the wine and 250 ml (8½ fl oz) of the stock, and stir in the tomato purée. Cover and cook over a very low heat until the rabbit is tender, about 15–20 minutes for boneless meat or 30 minutes for joints.

4 Remove the rabbit from the sauce and set it aside to cool. When cool enough to handle, cut the meat into small pieces or dice, discarding skin and bones, and set it aside again.

5 While the rabbit is cooling, increase the heat slightly and continue to simmer the sauce, adding the remaining stock in stages as it cooks. Simmer for about 30 minutes or until the sauce is reduced to a coating consistency and well flavoured.

6 Meanwhile, cook the pappardelle in boiling water for 10–12 minutes, or according to the packet instructions, until al dente.

7 Return the diced meat to the sauce and heat it through. Drain the pasta, transfer it to a serving dish and lightly toss with the remaining ½ tbsp olive oil. Top with the sauce and serve immediately with the Parmesan cheese.

Some more ideas

• Instead of rabbit, use boneless turkey breast, cut into large fillets, or chicken portions.

• If you can't find dried pappardelle, make your own by cutting sheets of fresh lasagne into 2 cm (¾ in) wide noodles (see page 19 for home-made pasta). Cook for 4–5 minutes or until al dente.

Plus points

• Rabbit is high in protein and relatively low in fat, the fat content being similar to skinned chicken. It is rich in B vitamins and a good source of iron.

• Red wine contains flavonoid compounds which may help to protect against heart disease.

especially good

146

Rotolo of ricotta and spinach

This is an attractive recipe to serve as a main dish, and it is equally good served as a first course, when it will provide 8 portions. Serve a fresh, crisp green salad as an accompaniment, taking advantage of the wide range of leaves and green vegetables that can be eaten raw.

Serves 4

8 sheets fresh lasagne verde, about 170 g (6 oz) in total (see page 19 for home-made pasta)

500 g (1 lb 2 oz) frozen chopped spinach, thawed

½ tbsp extra virgin olive oil

2 garlic cloves, chopped

85 g (3 oz) pancetta, chopped

225 g (8 oz) ricotta cheese

2 tbsp chopped mixed fresh herbs, such as parsley, thyme and oregano

¼ tsp freshly grated nutmeg

3 tbsp fresh breadcrumbs

3 tbsp freshly grated Parmesan cheese

salt and pepper

fresh oregano leaves to garnish

Red pepper sauce

1 large red pepper, halved and seeded

1 tsp extra virgin olive oil

2 garlic cloves, chopped

1 tbsp plain flour

240 ml (8 fl oz) chicken or vegetable stock

2 tomatoes, skinned, seeded and chopped

1 tbsp tomato purée

½ tsp sugar

Preparation time: 50 minutes
Cooking time: 20–25 minutes

1 Preheat the oven to 200°C (400°F, gas mark 6) and grease a shallow ovenproof dish.

2 Cook the lasagne in boiling water for 3–5 minutes, or according to the packet instructions, until al dente. Drain, rinse in cold water and drain again, then lay the sheets out on a clean tea-towel, in a single layer, to dry.

3 Drain the spinach thoroughly in a fine sieve, pressing out all the liquid with the back of a spoon.

4 Heat the oil in a heavy-based saucepan. Add the garlic and pancetta, and fry for 2 minutes. Stir in the spinach until thoroughly mixed, then leave to cool slightly.

5 Stir in the ricotta, herbs, nutmeg and seasoning to taste. Divide the filling equally among the sheets of lasagne, spreading it to the edges. Roll up each sheet like a Swiss roll and place in the prepared dish.

6 Mix the breadcrumbs with the cheese and sprinkle this over the rolls. Bake for 20–25 minutes or until brown and crisp.

7 Meanwhile, make the sauce. Preheat the grill to the hottest setting and grill the pepper halves, skin side up, until blistered and blackened. Cool in a polythene bag, then peel the peppers and chop them.

8 Heat the oil and fry the garlic and peppers for 2 minutes. Stir in the flour, then gradually pour in the stock, stirring all the time. Add the tomatoes, tomato purée, sugar and seasoning to taste. Stir well. Bring the sauce to the boil, then reduce the heat and cover the pan. Simmer for 10 minutes. Blend the sauce until smooth in a food processor or blender. Return the sauce to the pan and reheat it gently, stirring occasionally.

9 Cut each rotolo diagonally into 3 slices and arrange these on plates. Pour some of the sauce around the slices and serve the remainder separately. Garnish with oregano and serve immediately.

Plus points

• Not only is frozen spinach convenient and versatile, but it also retains almost 80% of its vitamin C content after 3 months of storage. This compares well to the fresh vegetable, which loses almost 50% of its vitamin C within 3 days when stored in the fridge.

especially good

Some more ideas

● Cook 340 g (12 oz) frozen peas in boiling water for 1 minute, drain and crush them with a potato masher. Mix in 1 tbsp chopped fresh thyme, or 1 tsp dried thyme, and the grated zest of 1 lemon. Use this pea mixture instead of the spinach in the rotolo filling.

● For a vegetarian version, simply omit the pancetta.

● For a sauce of diced vegetables, fry 2 finely diced carrots with the garlic and red peppers. Add 2 diced courgettes and 2 finely chopped spring onions after 5 minutes' cooking. Do not blend the sauce, but leave it chunky.

Each serving provides

kcal 495, **protein** 23 g, **fat** 22 g (of which saturated fat 9.5 g), **carbohydrate** 54 g (of which sugars 8 g), **fibre** 3 g

✓✓✓	A, calcium
✓✓	C, copper, potassium
✓	B_1, niacin, selenium

Stuffed giant pasta shells

A creamy sauce of courgettes, low-fat ricotta and walnuts reinterprets an Italian classic, and makes a wonderful, sophisticated dressing for pasta shells filled with a spinach and herb stuffing.

Serves 4

500 g (1 lb 2 oz) spinach, trimmed

3 courgettes, thinly sliced

4 garlic cloves, chopped

500 ml (17 fl oz) vegetable stock

250 g (9 oz) ricotta cheese

100 g (3½ oz) walnuts, coarsely chopped

85 g (3 oz) Parmesan cheese, freshly grated

3 tbsp chopped fresh chervil or marjoram

3 tbsp chopped fresh chives or 3 small
   shallots, finely chopped

3 tbsp chopped fresh basil

1 egg, lightly beaten

12 no-precook conchiglie grande (giant pasta
   shells for stuffing)

55 g (2 oz) Edam cheese, grated

2 tbsp finely shredded fresh basil or tiny basil
   leaves

salt and pepper

Preparation time: 40 minutes, plus 5 minutes
   standing

Cooking time: 30 minutes

Each serving provides ⓥ

kcal 630, **protein 34 g, fat 38 g** (of which
saturated fat 13 g), **carbohydrate 39 g** (of
which sugars 6 g), **fibre 5.5 g**

✓✓✓	A, calcium
✓✓	B₁, B₂, B₁₂, C, E, folate, niacin, copper, potassium
✓	B₆, iron, selenium

1 Wash the spinach well and place the wet leaves in a large saucepan. Cover and cook over a high heat for about 3 minutes, shaking the pan frequently. When the spinach is just tender and wilted, tip it into a colander and leave it to drain and cool.

2 Meanwhile, place the courgettes and half the garlic in a saucepan. Pour in the stock and bring to the boil. Cook over a high heat for about 3 minutes or until the courgettes are just tender.

3 Purée the courgettes and stock in a blender or food processor until smooth, adding half the ricotta cheese, the walnuts, 2 tbsp Parmesan cheese and seasoning to taste. The resulting sauce should have a consistency halfway between single and double cream, slightly more runny than a coating sauce should be.

4 When the spinach is cool enough to handle, squeeze it dry in small handfuls and chop it coarsely. Mix the spinach with the chervil or marjoram, chives or shallots, basil, the remaining garlic and ricotta cheese, the egg and seasoning to taste.

5 Preheat the oven to 190°C (375°F, gas mark 5). Use a small teaspoon to stuff the pasta shells with the spinach mixture, and arrange them in an ovenproof dish.

6 Pour the sauce over the stuffed shells and sprinkle with the remaining grated Parmesan. Cover the dish tightly with foil and bake for 30 minutes.

7 Sprinkle the Edam cheese and basil over the cooked stuffed pasta and leave to stand for 5 minutes, uncovered, until the cheese melts, then serve.

Some more ideas

● All sorts of greens can be used in this filling to replace some or all of the spinach and herbs. Try beet tops, Swiss chard, fresh borage and dandelion leaves. Raid your own herb garden or explore the greenery counter in the supermarket for exciting, vitamin-packed combinations.

Plus points

● Walnuts are a good source of polyunsaturated fat and essential fatty acids. Some studies indicate that eating a small quantity of walnuts daily combined with a low-fat diet can help to reduce high blood cholesterol levels. Walnuts also provide useful amounts of vitamin E, many of the B vitamins, potassium and protein.

especially good

Tagliatelle with mushroom medley

Choose a variety of exotic and wild mushrooms for this feast of fungi. Their flavours are complemented by rich Marsala in a dish that will fit perfectly into a well-balanced diet – the result is very pleasing without being laden with cream, the ingredient that usually makes mushroom sauces overrich.

Serves 4

10 g (¼ oz) dried porcini mushrooms

90 ml (3 fl oz) boiling water

2 tbsp extra virgin olive oil

3 shallots, chopped

225 g (8 oz) button or closed cap mushrooms, sliced

150 ml (5 fl oz) Marsala

450 g (1 lb) tagliatelle

1 garlic clove, finely chopped (optional)

450 g (1 lb) mixed mushrooms, such as shiitake, oyster, chestnut, chanterelle or other wild mushrooms, sliced or halved

250 g (9 oz) tomatoes, skinned, seeded and sliced

2 tsp fresh thyme leaves or 1 tsp dried thyme

2 tbsp chopped fresh parsley

salt and pepper

Preparation time: 15 minutes, plus 15 minutes soaking

Cooking time: 30 minutes

Each serving provides Ⓥ

kcal 534, **protein** 18 g, **fat** 9 g (of which saturated fat 1 g), **carbohydrate** 90 g (of which sugars 8 g), **fibre** 6.5 g

✓✓✓	copper
✓✓	niacin, potassium, selenium
✓	B$_1$, B$_2$, B$_6$, C, E, folate

1 Put the dried porcini mushrooms in a bowl and cover with the boiling water. Set aside to soak for 15 minutes, then drain, reserving the soaking liquid. Slice the rehydrated mushrooms, discarding any tough stalks.

2 Heat half the olive oil in a saucepan and fry the shallots until they are tender and golden, about 3 minutes. Add the button or closed cap mushrooms and cook for a further 8–10 minutes or until all the juice from the mushrooms has evaporated.

3 Add the Marsala and the soaking liquid from the dried mushrooms. Simmer for about 10 minutes or until the sauce has reduced by half.

4 Meanwhile, cook the tagliatelle in boiling water for 10–12 minutes, or according to the packet instructions, until al dente.

5 About 5 minutes before the pasta is done, heat the remaining 1 tbsp oil in a large frying pan. Add the garlic, if using, and the mixed mushrooms. Cook over a moderate heat for 3–5 minutes, shaking the pan often, until the mushrooms are lightly cooked.

6 Stir the tomatoes, thyme and parsley into the mushroom sauce and heat through for 1–2 minutes. Add the mixed mushrooms, season to taste and remove from the heat.

7 Drain the tagliatelle and divide it among 4 serving dishes. Spoon the mushroom sauce on top and serve immediately.

Some more ideas

• For a creamy sauce, stir in 4 tbsp of fromage frais or Greek-style yogurt with the tomatoes.

• White or red wine can be used in place of the Marsala.

Plus points

• Mushrooms are a useful source of the B vitamins niacin, B$_6$ and folate, and they provide a good source of copper, one of the all-important minerals that form part of a healthy diet.

• Most recipes use mushrooms in small quantities, so that the nutritional contribution they make to the diet is limited. However, the dish here contains a substantial amount of fresh mushrooms, plus dried ones for additional flavour.

especially good

153

Couscous pilaf with tahini yogurt

This vegetable-rich couscous is lower in fat than most pilafs and it makes a marvellous, healthy main dish, or an excellent side dish for almost any simply cooked meat or poultry, when it will serve 8 or more. Any leftovers can be used as a delicious stuffing for chicken or other poultry or game birds.

especially good

Serves 6

1 tbsp extra virgin olive oil
1 medium or 2 small onions, chopped
4 garlic cloves, chopped
1 small carrot, diced
1 tsp mild chilli powder
1 tsp ground coriander
1 tsp garam masala
2½ tsp paprika
½ tsp ground ginger
½ tsp ground cinnamon
2½ tsp ground cumin
4 green cardamom pods
85 g (3 oz) sweet potato, cut into chunks
85 g (3 oz) turnip, diced
1 courgette, cut into bite-sized chunks
75 g (2½ oz) runner or French beans
1 can chopped tomatoes, about 400 g
900 ml (1½ pints) vegetable stock
1 can borlotti beans, about 400 g, drained
250 g (9 oz) cabbage, roughly chopped
85 g (3 oz) broccoli, cut into small florets
340 g (12 oz) couscous
3 tbsp sultanas
salt and pepper

Tahini yogurt

2 tbsp tahini
4 tbsp plain low-fat yogurt
1 tbsp lemon juice
fresh coriander to garnish

Preparation time: 25 minutes
Cooking time: 35 minutes

1 Heat the oil in a 4.5 litre (8 pint) stockpot, flameproof casserole or saucepan and add the onion. Reserve the equivalent of about 1 garlic clove, then add the rest to the pan. Cook for about 3 minutes or until the onion has softened slightly. Add the carrot and cook for another 3 minutes.

2 Sprinkle in the chilli powder, coriander, garam masala, paprika, ginger, cinnamon and 2 tsp cumin (reserve the remaining cumin for the tahini yogurt). Split the cardamom pods and scrape the tiny black seeds into the pan. Stir for a few seconds, then add the sweet potato, turnip and courgette. Cut the beans into bite-sized lengths and add to the pan. Cook the vegetables for 5 minutes or until softened slightly.

3 Pour in the tomatoes with their juice and the stock, and stir in the borlotti beans. Bring to the boil, then reduce the heat, cover and simmer for 10–15 minutes. Add the cabbage and broccoli, and cook, covered, for a further 5 minutes.

4 Reduce the heat to the lowest setting. Add the couscous and sultanas with seasoning to taste. Fork through the vegetables and stock. Cover and cook very gently for 5 minutes. The couscous should have absorbed all the liquid and plumped up.

5 Meanwhile, make the tahini yogurt. (Stir the tahini in the jar to ensure it is smooth before measuring out the quantity for the recipe.) Mix the tahini with the reserved garlic and the yogurt, then stir in 4 tbsp water, the lemon juice, the reserved ½ tsp ground cumin and seasoning to taste. Sprinkle with coriander leaves to garnish.

6 Serve the pilaf with the tahini yogurt offered separately.

Plus points

• Borlotti beans are low in fat and rich in carbohydrate. They provide good amounts of B vitamins (B_1, niacin and B_6) and useful amounts of iron. In common with other beans and pulses, they are a good source of fibre, particularly soluble fibre, which can help to reduce high blood cholesterol levels.

• Broccoli is an excellent source of beta-carotene and vitamins C and E. It also provides good amounts of the B vitamins niacin, folate and B_6.

Some more ideas

● Use pumpkin or winter squash, such as butternut or acorn squash, instead of sweet potato, and raisins instead of sultanas. Use swede instead of turnip.

● Many other beans and pulses are delicious in this pilaf, in particular canned or soaked and cooked chickpeas.

● A chilli sauce, such as the Moroccan harissa, could be offered with the pilaf for those who like hot flavours.

Each serving provides　Ⓥ

kcal 330, **protein** 13 g, **fat** 6.5 g (of which saturated fat 1 g), **carbohydrate** 57 g (of which sugars 15 g), **fibre** 8 g

✓✓	A, B_1, C, calcium, potassium
✓	B_6, E, niacin, iron

A glossary of nutritional terms

Antioxidants These are compounds that help to protect the body's cells against the damaging effects of free radicals. Vitamins C and E, beta-carotene (the plant form of vitamin A) and the mineral selenium, together with many of the phytochemicals found in fruit and vegetables, all act as antioxidants.

Calorie A unit used to measure the energy value of food and the intake and use of energy by the body. The scientific definition of 1 calorie is the amount of heat required to raise the temperature of 1 gram of water by 1 degree Centigrade. This is such a small amount that in this country we tend to use the term kilocalories (abbreviated to *kcal*), which is equivalent to 1000 calories. Energy values can also be measured in kilojoules (kJ): 1 kcal = 4.2 kJ.

A person's energy (calorie) requirement varies depending on his or her age, sex and level of activity. The estimated average daily energy requirements are:

Age (years)	Female (kcal)	Male (kcal)
1–3	1165	1230
4–6	1545	1715
7–10	1740	1970
11–14	1845	2220
15–18	2110	2755
19–49	1940	2550
50–59	1900	2550
60–64	1900	2380
65–74	1900	2330

Carbohydrates These energy-providing substances are present in varying amounts in different foods and are found in three main forms: sugars, starches and non-starch polysaccharides (NSP), usually called fibre.

There are two types of sugars: *intrinsic sugars*, which occur naturally in fruit (fructose) and sweet-tasting vegetables, and *extrinsic sugars*, which include lactose (from milk) and all the non-milk extrinsic sugars (NMEs) – sucrose (table sugar), honey, treacle, molasses and so on. The NMEs, or 'added' sugars, provide only calories, whereas foods containing intrinsic sugars also offer vitamins, minerals and fibre. Added sugars (*simple carbohydrates*) are digested and absorbed rapidly to provide energy very quickly. Starches and fibre (*complex carbohydrates*), on the other hand, break down more slowly to offer a longer-term energy source (see also Glycaemic Index). Starchy carbohydrates are found in bread, pasta, rice,

wholegrain and breakfast cereals, and potatoes and other starchy vegetables such as parsnips, sweet potatoes and yams.

Healthy eating guidelines recommend that at least half of our daily energy (calories) should come from carbohydrates, and that most of this should be from complex carbohydrates. No more than 11% of our total calorie intake should come from 'added' sugars. For an average woman aged 19–49 years, this would mean a total carbohydrate intake of 259 g per day, of which 202 g should be from starch and intrinsic sugars and no more than 57 g from added sugars. For a man of the same age, total carbohydrates each day should be about 340 g (265 g from starch and intrinsic sugars and 75 g from added sugars).

See also Fibre and Glycogen.

Cholesterol There are two types of cholesterol – the soft waxy substance called blood cholesterol, which is an integral part of human cell membranes, and dietary cholesterol, which is contained in food. *Blood cholesterol* is important in the formation of some hormones and it aids digestion. High blood cholesterol levels are known to be an important risk factor for coronary heart disease, but most of the cholesterol in our blood is made by the liver – only about 25% comes from cholesterol in food. So while it would seem that the amount of cholesterol-rich foods in the diet would have a direct effect on blood cholesterol levels, in fact the best way to reduce blood cholesterol is to eat less saturated fat and to increase intake of foods containing soluble fibre.

Fat Although a small amount of fat is essential for good health, most people consume far too much. Healthy eating guidelines recommend that no more than 33% of our daily energy intake (calories) should come from fat. Each gram of fat contains 9 kcal, more than twice as many calories as carbohydrate or protein, so for a woman aged 19–49 years this means a daily maximum of 71 g fat, and for a man in the same age range 93.5 g fat.

Fats can be divided into 3 main groups: saturated, monounsaturated and polyunsaturated, depending on the chemical structure of the fatty acids they contain. *Saturated fatty acids* are found mainly in animal fats such as butter and other dairy products and in fatty meat. A high intake of saturated fat is known to be a risk factor for coronary heart disease and certain types of cancer. Current guidelines are that no more than 10% of our daily calories should come from saturated fats, which is about 21.5 g for an adult woman and 28.5 g for a man.

Where saturated fats tend to be solid at room temperature, the *unsaturated fatty acids* –

monounsaturated and polyunsaturated – tend to be liquid. *Monounsaturated fats* are found predominantly in olive oil, groundnut (peanut) oil, rapeseed oil and avocados. Foods high in *polyunsaturates* include most vegetable oils – the exceptions are palm oil and coconut oil, both of which are saturated.

Both saturated and monounsaturated fatty acids can be made by the body, but certain polyunsaturated fatty acids – known as *essential fatty acids* – must be supplied by food. There are 2 'families' of these essential fatty acids: *omega-6*, derived from linoleic acid, and *omega-3*, from linolenic acid. The main food sources of the omega-6 family are vegetable oils such as olive and sunflower; omega-3 fatty acids are provided by oily fish, nuts, and vegetable oils such as soya and rapeseed.

When vegetable oils are hydrogenated (hardened) to make margarine and reduced-fat spreads, their unsaturated fatty acids can be changed into trans fatty acids, or '*trans fats*'. These artificially produced trans fats are believed to act in the same way as saturated fats within the body – with the same risks to health. Current healthy eating guidelines suggest that no more than 2% of our daily calories should come from trans fats, which is about 4.3 g for an adult woman and 5.6 g for a man. In thinking about the amount of trans fats you consume, remember that major sources are processed foods such as biscuits, pies, cakes and crisps.

Fibre Technically non-starch polysaccharides (NSP), fibre is the term commonly used to describe several different compounds, such as pectin, hemicellulose, lignin and gums, which are found in the cell walls of all plants. The body cannot digest fibre, nor does it have much nutritional value, but it plays an important role in helping us to stay healthy.

Fibre can be divided into 2 groups – soluble and insoluble. Both types are provided by most plant foods, but some foods are particularly good sources of one type or the other. *Soluble fibre* (in oats, pulses, fruit and vegetables) can help to reduce high blood cholesterol levels and to control blood sugar levels by slowing down the absorption of sugar. *Insoluble fibre* (in wholegrain cereals, pulses, fruit and vegetables) increases stool bulk and speeds the passage of waste material through the body. In this way it helps to prevent constipation, haemorrhoids and diverticular disease, and may protect against bowel cancer.

Our current intake of fibre is around 12 g a day. Healthy eating guidelines suggest that we need to increase this amount to 18 g a day.

Free radicals These highly reactive molecules can cause damage to cell walls and DNA (the genetic material found within cells). They are believed to be involved in the development of heart disease, some cancers and premature ageing. Free radicals are produced naturally by

glossary

the body in the course of everyday life, but certain factors, such as cigarette smoke, pollution and over-exposure to sunlight, can accelerate their production.

Gluten A protein found in wheat and, to a lesser degree, in rye, barley and oats, but not in corn (maize) or rice. People with *coeliac disease* have a sensitivity to gluten and need to eliminate all gluten-containing foods, such as bread, pasta, cakes and biscuits, from their diet.

Glycaemic Index (GI) This is used to measure the rate at which carbohydrate foods are digested and converted into sugar (glucose) to raise blood sugar levels and provide energy. Foods with a high GI are quickly broken down and offer an immediate energy fix, while those with a lower GI are absorbed more slowly, making you feel full for longer and helping to keep blood sugar levels constant. High-GI foods include table sugar, honey, mashed potatoes and watermelon. Low-GI foods include pulses, wholewheat cereals, apples, cherries, dried apricots, pasta and oats.

Glycogen This is one of the 2 forms in which energy from carbohydrates is made available for use by the body (the other is *glucose*). Whereas glucose is converted quickly from carbohydrates and made available in the blood for a fast energy fix, glycogen is stored in the liver and muscles to fuel longer-term energy needs. When the body has used up its immediate supply of glucose, the stored glycogen is broken down into glucose to continue supplying energy.

Minerals These inorganic substances perform a wide range of vital functions in the body. The *macrominerals* – calcium, chloride, magnesium, potassium, phosphorus and sodium – are needed in relatively large quantities, whereas much smaller amounts are required of the remainder, called *microminerals*. Some microminerals (selenium, magnesium and iodine, for example) are needed in such tiny amounts that they are known as *'trace elements'*.

There are important differences in the body's ability to absorb minerals from different foods, and this can be affected by the presence of other substances. For example, oxalic acid, present in spinach, interferes with the absorption of much of the iron and calcium spinach contains.
• *Calcium* is essential for the development of strong bones and teeth. It also plays an important role in blood clotting. Good sources include dairy products, canned fish (eaten with their bones) and dark green, leafy vegetables.
• *Chloride* helps to maintain the body's fluid balance. The main source in the diet is table salt.
• *Chromium* is important in the regulation of blood sugar levels, as well as levels of fat and cholesterol in the blood. Good dietary sources include red meat, liver, eggs, seafood, cheese and wholegrain cereals.

• *Copper*, component of many enzymes, is needed for bone growth and the formation of connective tissue. It helps the body to absorb iron from food. Good sources include offal, shellfish, mushrooms, cocoa, nuts and seeds.
• *Iodine* is an important component of the thyroid hormones, which govern the rate and efficiency at which food is converted into energy. Good sources include seafood, seaweed and vegetables (depending on the iodine content of the soil in which they are grown).
• *Iron* is an essential component of haemoglobin, the pigment in red blood cells that carries oxygen around the body. Good sources are offal, red meat, dried apricots and prunes, and iron-fortified breakfast cereals.
• *Magnesium* is important for healthy bones, the release of energy from food, and nerve and muscle function. Good sources include wholegrain cereals, peas and other green vegetables, pulses, dried fruit and nuts.
• *Manganese* is a vital component of several enzymes that are involved in energy production and many other functions. Good dietary sources include nuts, cereals, brown rice, pulses and wholemeal bread.
• *Molybdenum* is an essential component of several enzymes, including those involved in the production of DNA. Good sources are offal, yeast, pulses, wholegrain cereals and green leafy vegetables.
• *Phosphorus* is important for healthy bones and teeth and for the release of energy from foods. It is found in most foods. Particularly good sources include dairy products, red meat, poultry, fish and eggs.
• *Potassium*, along with sodium, is important in maintaining fluid balance and regulating blood pressure, and is essential for the transmission of nerve impulses. Good sources include fruit, especially bananas and citrus fruits, nuts, seeds, potatoes and pulses.
• *Selenium* is a powerful antioxidant that protects cells against damage by free radicals. Good dietary sources are meat, fish, dairy foods, brazil nuts, avocados and lentils.
• *Sodium* works with potassium to regulate fluid balance, and is essential for nerve and muscle function. Only a little sodium is needed – we tend to get too much in our diet. The main source in the diet is table salt, as well as salty processed foods and ready-prepared foods.
• *Sulphur* is a component of 2 essential amino acids. Protein foods are the main source.
• *Zinc* is vital for normal growth, as well as reproduction and immunity. Good dietary sources include oysters, red meat, peanuts and sunflower seeds.

Phytochemicals These biologically active compounds, found in most plant foods, are believed to be beneficial in disease prevention. There are literally thousands of different phytochemicals, amongst which are the following:

• *Allicin*, a phytochemical found in garlic, onions, leeks, chives and shallots, is believed to help lower high blood cholesterol levels and stimulate the immune system.
• *Bioflavonoids*, of which there are at least 6000, are found mainly in fruit and sweet-tasting vegetables. Different bioflavonoids have different roles – some are antioxidants, while others act as anti-disease agents. A sub-group of these phytochemicals, called *flavonols*, includes the antioxidant *quercetin*, which is believed to reduce the risk of heart disease and help to protect against cataracts. Quercetin is found in tea, red wine, grapes and broad beans.
• *Carotenoids*, the best known of which are *beta-carotene* and *lycopene*, are powerful antioxidants thought to help protect us against certain types of cancer. Highly coloured fruits and vegetables, such as blackcurrants, mangoes, tomatoes, carrots, sweet potatoes, pumpkin and dark green, leafy vegetables, are excellent sources of carotenoids.
• *Coumarins* are believed to help protect against cancer by inhibiting the formation of tumours. Oranges are a rich source.
• *Glucosinolates*, found mainly in cruciferous vegetables, particularly broccoli, Brussels sprouts, cabbage, kale and cauliflower, are believed to have strong anti-cancer effects. *Sulphoraphane* is one of the powerful cancer-fighting substances produced by glucosinolates.
• *Phytoestrogens* have a chemical structure similar to the female hormone oestrogen, and they are believed to help protect against hormone-related cancers such as breast and prostate cancer. One of the types of these phytochemicals, called *isoflavones*, may also help to relieve symptoms associated with the menopause. Soya beans and chickpeas are a particularly rich source of isoflavones.

Protein This nutrient, necessary for growth and development, for maintenance and repair of cells, and for the production of enzymes, antibodies and hormones, is essential to keep the body working efficiently. Protein is made up of *amino acids*, which are compounds containing the 4 elements that are necessary for life: carbon, hydrogen, oxygen and nitrogen. We need all of the 20 amino acids commonly found in plant and animal proteins. The human body can make 12 of these, but the remaining 8 – called *essential amino acids* – must be obtained from the food we eat.

Protein comes in a wide variety of foods. Meat, fish, dairy products, eggs and soya beans contain all of the essential amino acids, and are therefore called first-class protein foods. Pulses, nuts, seeds and cereals are also good sources of protein, but do not contain the full range of essential amino acids. In practical terms, this really doesn't matter – as long as you include a variety of different protein foods in your diet, your body will get all the amino acids it needs. It is important, though, to eat protein foods every day because the essential amino acids cannot be stored in the body for later use.

The RNI of protein for women aged 19–49 years is 45 g per day and for men of the same age 55 g. In the UK most people eat more protein than they need, although this isn't normally a problem.

Reference Nutrient Intake (RNI) This denotes the average daily amount of vitamins and minerals thought to be sufficient to meet the nutritional needs of almost all individuals within the population. The figures, published by the Department of Health, vary depending on age, sex and specific nutritional needs such as pregnancy. RNIs are equivalent to what used to be called Recommended Daily Amounts or Allowances (RDA).

RNIs for adults (19–49 years)

Vitamin A	600–700 mcg
Vitamin B_1	0.8 mg for women, 1 mg for men
Vitamin B_2	1.1 mg for women, 1.3 mg for men
Niacin	13 mg for women, 17 mg for men
Vitamin B_6	1.2 mg for women, 1.4 mg for men
Vitamin B_{12}	1.5 mg
Folate	200 mcg (400 mcg for first trimester of pregnancy)
Vitamin C	40 mg
Vitamin E	no recommendation in the UK; the EC RDA is 10 mg, which has been used in all recipe analyses in this book
Calcium	700 mg
Chloride	2500 mg
Copper	1.2 mg
Iodine	140 mcg
Iron	14.8 mg for women, 8.7 mg for men
Magnesium	270–300 mg
Phosphorus	550 mg
Potassium	3500 mg
Selenium	60 mcg for women, 75 mcg for men
Sodium	1600 mg
Zinc	7 mg for women, 9.5 mg for men

Vitamins These are organic compounds that are essential for good health. Although they are required in only small amounts, each one has specific vital functions to perform. Most vitamins cannot be made by the human body, and therefore must be obtained from the diet. The body is capable of storing some vitamins (A, D, E, K and B_{12}), but the rest need to be provided by the diet on a regular basis. A well-balanced diet, containing a wide variety of different foods, is the best way to ensure that you get all the vitamins you need.

Vitamins can be divided into 2 groups: *water-soluble* (B complex and C) and *fat-soluble* (A, D, E and K). Water-soluble vitamins are easily destroyed during processing, storage, and the preparation and cooking of food. The fat-soluble vitamins are less vulnerable to losses during cooking and processing.

• *Vitamin A* (retinol) is essential for healthy vision, eyes, skin and growth. Good sources include dairy products, offal (especially liver), eggs and oily fish. Vitamin A can also be obtained from *beta-carotene*, the pigment found in highly coloured fruit and vegetables. In addition to acting as a source of vitamin A, beta-carotene has an important role to play as an antioxidant in its own right.

• *The B Complex vitamins* have very similar roles to play in nutrition, and many of them occur together in the same foods.
Vitamin B_1 (thiamin) is essential in the release of energy from carbohydrates. Good sources include milk, offal, meat (especially pork), wholegrain and fortified breakfast cereals, nuts and pulses, yeast extract and wheat germ. White flour and bread are fortified with B_1 in the UK.
Vitamin B_2 (riboflavin) is vital for growth, healthy skin and eyes, and the release of energy from food. Good sources include milk, meat, offal, eggs, cheese, fortified breakfast cereals, yeast extract and green leafy vegetables.
Niacin (nicotinic acid), sometimes called vitamin B_3, plays an important role in the release of energy within the cells. Unlike the other B vitamins it can be made by the body from the essential amino acid tryptophan. Good sources include meat, offal, fish, fortified breakfast cereals and pulses. White flour and bread are fortified with niacin in the UK.
Pantothenic acid, sometimes called vitamin B_5, is involved in a number of metabolic reactions, including energy production. This vitamin is present in most foods; notable exceptions are fat, oil and sugar. Good sources include liver, kidneys, yeast, egg yolks, fish roe, wheat germ, nuts, pulses and fresh vegetables.
Vitamin B_6 (pyridoxine) helps the body to utilise protein and contributes to the formation of haemoglobin for red blood cells. B_6 is found in a wide range of foods including meat, liver, fish, eggs, wholegrain cereals, some vegetables, pulses, brown rice, nuts and yeast extract.
Vitamin B_{12} (cyanocobalamin) is vital for growth, the formation of red blood cells and maintenance of a healthy nervous system. B_{12} is unique in that it is only found in foods of animal origin. Vegetarians who eat dairy products will get enough, but vegans need to ensure they include food fortified with B_{12} in their diet. Good sources of B_{12} include liver, kidneys, oily fish, meat, cheese, eggs and milk.
Folate (folic acid) is involved in the manufacture of amino acids and in the production of red blood cells. Recent research suggests that folate may also help to protect against heart disease. Good sources of folate are green leafy vegetables, liver, pulses, eggs, wholegrain cereal products and fortified breakfast cereals, brewers' yeast, wheatgerm, nuts and fruit, especially grapefruit and oranges.
Biotin is needed for various metabolic reactions and the release of energy from foods. Good sources include liver, oily fish, brewers' yeast, kidneys, egg yolks and brown rice.

• *Vitamin C* (ascorbic acid) is essential for growth and vital for the formation of collagen (a protein needed for healthy bones, teeth, gums, blood capillaries and all connective tissue). It plays an important role in the healing of wounds and fractures, and acts as a powerful antioxidant. Vitamin C is found mainly in fruit and vegetables.

• *Vitamin D* (cholecalciferol) is essential for growth and the absorption of calcium, and thus for the formation of healthy bones. It is also involved in maintaining a healthy nervous system. The amount of vitamin D occurring naturally in foods is small, and it is found in very few foods – good sources are oily fish (and fish liver oil supplements), eggs and liver, as well as breakfast cereals, margarine and full-fat milk that are fortified with vitamin D. Most vitamin D, however, does not come from the diet but is made by the body when the skin is exposed to sunlight.

• *Vitamin E* is not one vitamin, but a number of related compounds called tocopherols that function as antioxidants. Good sources of vitamin E are vegetable oils, polyunsaturated margarines, wheatgerm, sunflower seeds, nuts, oily fish, eggs, wholegrain cereals, avocados and spinach.

• *Vitamin K* is essential for the production of several proteins, including prothombin which is involved in the clotting of blood. It has been found to exist in 3 forms, one of which is obtained from food while the other 2 are made by the bacteria in the intestine. Vitamin K_1, which is the form found in food, is present in broccoli, cabbage, spinach, milk, margarine, vegetable oils, particularly soya oil, cereals, liver, alfalfa and kelp.

Nutritional analyses

The nutritional analysis of each recipe has been carried out using data from *The Composition of Foods* with additional data from food manufacturers where appropriate. Because the level and availability of different nutrients can vary, depending on factors like growing conditions and breed of animal, the figures are intended as an approximate guide only.

The analyses include vitamins A, B_1, B_2, B_6, B_{12}, niacin, folate, C, D and E, and the minerals calcium, copper, iron, potassium, selenium and zinc. Other vitamins and minerals are not included as deficiencies are rare. Optional ingredients and optional serving suggestions have not been included in the calculations.

glossary

Index

index

Printing and binding: Printer Industria Gráfica S.A., Barcelona
Separations: Litho Origination, London
Paper: Périgord-Condat, France